# Thank You Guillain-Barré Syndrome

Rasith Asokan

*Translated from the Malayalam by*
Yoosaph Perambra

First Published in English in India by Emerald
(An Imprint of WINCO BOOKS)
Kottayam, Kerala, India
+91 9495856844
wincobooks@gmail.com
wincobooks.com



First English Edition 2021



Thank You Guillain-Barré Syndrome
By Rasith Asokan

English Edition of the Malayalam book
*Nanni Guillain-Barré Syndrome*

**ISBN 13: 978-81-948738-6-0**

WBIN: 2191431521067***

Cover Design by BrandMithra
Typesetting and Layout by Winco Publishing Services
Printed and bound in India

**India – ₹ 199 | Out of India – US $ 10 | UK £ 7**

# Prologue: A story of survival

*THANK YOU GUILLAIN-BARRE SYNDROME* is not a work of fiction. It is based on real-life experiences of Guillain-Barre Syndrome (GBS).

Again, this book is not about GBS. It is a story of survival and hope, faith and determination, a journey to a successful life facing the challenges.

It is the story of Rasith Asokan, a young man who was diagnosed with GBS. And his life took him in a direction he never saw himself going, but it turns out to be the best road he has ever taken.

We are never given anything we cannot handle. What we do with each challenge and how we move forward is what matters. The biggest challenge of Rasith's life was GBS. His desire to overcome this terrible disease, to battle it with dignity, and write a book about real-life experiences of GBS has proven to be an inspiration to many people.

The book was first published in Malayalam in October 2015. Within a short period, the book was reprinted 22 times and thousands of copies were sold, making it a national bestseller.

Winco Books is happy to publish the English edition of this book, and I am sure the English book will be well-received and will become another bestseller.

**Sabin John**
Winco Books

# Foreword: A concentration camp called the hospital

ONLY THOSE who do not submit to fatal sickness can heartily amuse themselves in the multicolour of the horizon, gentle wind, mild snow, and the mellowed voice of nightingales. When a patient gets startled himself in the thoughts of why he got an indisposition, he starts to drown in the fiery tentacles of it in a little while. Against the above notion, this short depiction of experiences illustrates his gentle confidence, positivity, mental stability and mild heart.

Writing is a blessed solitude. This book, therefore, smells of aesthetic perfume made from raw pain beaded with the petals of mind from the solitary island of sickness. Rasith never raises his eyebrows against his indisposition. He enjoys his situation with the amusement of a joker. He doesn't find time to blame anyone anywhere. Nor is he desolate. With a gentle smile, Rasith wanted to return from his indisposition that befell him as if in a flash of lightning when he was wholly immersed in the intoxication of life. That experience has been portrayed in the words spelt out in the book.

The one who had hard experiences in life cannot usually illustrate them in words. I am amazed at the way Rasith attempted to illustrate lucidly the experiences while undergoing treatment without an inch of pride in doing so. Pneumonia is the harbinger of death in the case of a patient in bed. This is the story of survival. A youth whose life was like a blossomed tree, all of a sudden gets emaciated in a fine morning, hands and fingers get paralysed, legs and limbs rendered still, loses his voice and appetite together, breathes with the support of a ventilator, high dosed antibiotic injected through the vein. The spine breaking hospital expenses for a middle-class family and a year-long hospital life. Even when he was strangled by fate like a coiling python, he did not lose his flowery smile. He went on listening to the flute of hope and confidence among all these. No one else can do this. Rasith was saved by his fearlessness.

The breezy memories of campus life sprinkled its elixir into his mind. He saw a wide canvas of campus life somewhere in a distant land. He saw only loving smiles around him. We find relief when Rasith slowly breathes back to life with the loving care of others while the entire world is gasping for it. The world of letters created by him becomes an unforgettable experience due to its ethereal fragrance of hope and universal life sprayed into the minds of every reader.

During the 31 years of my life with a broken spine, after reading Rasith's experiences I was filled with the fear of reality for the first time. I put myself in place of Rasith. Through the use of the words like 'angels', the readers and patients in ICU were relieved. The technical jargons used in the book are not familiar to us. Instead, they become the real experience of our own life. While his body was sinking day by day, he turned every moment into a joke and narrated the frightening moments to others as a joker. Thus, the writer describes his experience of being a patient at Baby Memorial Hospital, and he imbues the readers with pain and silence. Only a greatly talented writer can render this possible. This book is full of words written by the heart blood of the one with an emaciated body and wounded mind that would surely evoke hope and enthusiasm. Such is the language and narrative hitherto unknown in Malayalam literature.

A book of literature has to be an experience to the reader. Rasith could make it possible especially when it recounts the role of an indisposed. Rasith's magic of words will inundate the heart of the readers with crystal clear water even after they put the book down.

I believe that a work of literature has two essential factors: form and content. Not even a single line can be struck off from Rasith's work as unwanted in this respect. That means Rasith possesses his style of literature as a legacy. The content of this language is like the winding ladder to one's inner self. When the fragrant letters creep up this circular ladder, Malayalam language cannot forget this book.

*P.S.:* If this book had been concluded with the chapter 'Again to BMH', it would not have been possible for me to write this foreword. This part is so intense. My spine, liver, lungs and heart were fatally wounded on the 14 October 1983, and I was not able to even sit up on the bed as my feet were paralysed. The inflammation of the spine from T4 began to go up to T3. I fell into a state of insanity due to hallucination. Due to the inability of my limbs, I couldn't eat with my hands. I wanted to sit up on the bed. Both hands were engaged; one used for blood transfusion and the other for drip. Liquid food was given through my nose. Unable to urinate and defecate, it was catheterized. To solve the issue of constipation, doctors advised colostomy. 10-year-long fever, two years of drip-drop of urine, long months of hospitalisation, chest infection, cough, and tireless run of the angels. The relentless scream of the relatives of the dead.

Each word of Rasith recalled the state of my fatally bedridden life, and the intense smell of medicines, the hasty steps of angels and doctors' periodic rounds, commenting on the imminence of death. As Rasith says, everything revolved and finally reached a state of a sphere-like object. There remained a short ray of hope. Something moved as faint shadows. Suddenly, the light went off. Pitch darkness everywhere. Silence and deep darkness. I had lain in the concentration camp of the so-called hospital for recuperation.

Rasith too had a similar experience. There he had undergone intense pain through which finally he came back to life slowly putting his feet on like a messenger from heaven. Let us prostrate ourselves before him by dedicating thousands of flowers.

Simon Britto

# Preface: My second life

THE MODERN generation is going through muddled thoughts. The society is reluctant to identify their mental stress, support them, direct them and correct them. The young people resume their journey aimlessly to find a way of survival. And they conclude themselves that their life was a failure. In the middle of their wanderings to locate the sound waves named 'victory' imposed on their lives since their primary education, their thoughts, ideas, skills and creativity lose or get abandoned.

Even when GBS was partially successful in conquering my life at the ICU for about 4.5 months, it helped me to recover the abandoned thoughts and literary spirit. Find a boundary to the word victory or else enjoyment in life would be impossible. My journey today is along the beautiful path of creativity.

The day and night spent in the frozen ICU flickered in mind as if in a dream. I felt a hiccup when I could not join letters together with my hands. I should write, however. At last, I began to scribble the thoughts and memories on to the cell phone gifted by my intimate college mates. The bunch of shadows that move through our lives, sometimes, constantly haunt us throughout our lives. Some others shine through life. Sometimes such shadows get concretised as self-images in the depth of friendship. My bosom friend Jomol Joy came up to move her fingers for the crystallisation of the ideas into words. I forwarded her the scribbled pages to realise my dream named "Thank You Guillain-Barre Syndrome".

I place on record my esteemed gratitude to several dignitaries who joined hands with me in beading together the broken memories into this rosary of letters. First of all Dr. Alexander, Managing Director, Baby Memorial Hospital; Dr. V.G. Pradeep Kumar, who brought me back to life with his consoling words and medicines, monitoring the fluctuations in my blood pressure; Dr. Anoop Kumar A.S., Neuro ICU in-charge Sheena; Deshabhimani Chief Sub-Editor N.S. Sajith, who gave me a hand in beautifying my thoughts with necessary correction and editing (of course, after reading it completely); Smija P.S., Ramanattukara Seva Mandir Post Basic Higher Secondary School teacher; my college mates of CKGM College, Perambra; my school mates; above all, to every true being who stretched their hands and hearts to save and bring me back to my second life.

Words are like fire-wicked spears. The forgotten nostalgic letters put their hands on my shoulders and escort me slowly into life. It was at a time when I fell from the height to a wide zero, the big and beautiful circle of the big zero became clearer. This big zero taught me the lesson that the failed and victorious have also their space in life, but staying back like a defeated has no room in history.

Dear all, thank you very much for reading this real experience and for your encouragement in making this book a great success that enabled to reach its 22nd edition in Malayalam.

The frequent call came to a standstill suddenly ... "Rasith ... I'm at the Guest House, Perambra ... meet me here when you're free ..." The dearest Simon Britto departed ... when oxygen, food and water reach our body, our physical organs and cells start functioning ... life is the product of the joint energy created by this process.

Then where is the mind? Inside the body or outside? Britto looked at my face for a long time, then laughed wildly ... Britto has departed ... Forever ... No ... He will not call me anymore ... Two orphaned slippers remain uncared for in the 'Kayam' of Vaduthala ...

Rasith Asokan

# Contents


1. Bengaluru ... 12
2. Mysuru ... 15
3. What happened to this man? ... 22
4. To Kerala ... 30
5. Baby Memorial Hospital ... 34
6. ICU ... 37
7. Angels of BMH ... 46
8. Life breath ... 56
9. Tracheostomy ... 60
10. Ventilator again ... 65
11. Bronchoscopy ... 76
12. Again to BMH ... 86
13. Face to face with death ... 93
14. To Mundakkutty ... 101
15. Physiotherapy ... 106
16. She was waiting for me ... 112
17. On the shore of my love ... 120

# 1. Bengaluru

BENGALURU 2013. A drizzling morning in June. To reach the chitty company Sree Gokulam Chit & Finance Company in Gandhi Nagar took at least one hour on a bike from my residence. My raincoat was on; still, the body was more drenched than I expected due to the freezing raindrops that pierced into my body. It was with a turbulent mind that I began to climb the stairs of my office. I had received unconfirmed information that it was transfer time again.

Perhaps it would be because of my strayed habit. Moving out of my designated authority, I had started to utilise qualitatively my knowledge and experience. Such moments, as I know, would pave way for the dislikes from others; yet I was never ready to backtrack on my actions. Unable to judge positively or negatively on my present behaviour, I had been getting on real achievements alone. Promotions, handsome amounts of perks, etc.

I forgot to tell you. It was on the first day of September 2005 that I got connected with Sree Gokulam Chit & Finance Company. The interview was held at the headquarters of Gokulam at Kodambakkam in Chennai. I had to reach there on Monday. So I started on Saturday itself. Mangalore-Chennai Express reached the Central Railway station in the early morning.

The jasmine smelling Tamil streets were slowly awakening. A group of joyous people dancing and singing could be seen passing through the street behind Pachaiyappa's College near Bagi Akka's (auntie's) house. The mood of celebration now has shifted to another scene in which they were bearing the dead body of a Tamilian in the neighbourhood. I saw that death was a celebration for them. Finishing a hasty shower bath, we set off to meet the chairman of the Gokulam Group of companies A.M. Gopalan (Gokulam Gopalan), on the two-wheeler of my friend Vinod.

By the time we reached near the gate of his house, he had set on a morning walk. When I told him about my desire to talk to him, he returned to his house followed by us. We got a hospitable reception, were served breakfast, and he also booked accommodation in a nearby hotel. Then he left home to resume his morning walk. After the successful completion of all the tests that were conducted the next day, I caught a train to my homeland. The contented mind also joined the beautiful sights that seemed to be moving outside the train window.

The initial appointment was in the chilly Jayanagar of Bengaluru. Taming Kannada language, learning the mantra of success in my career, I was trying to survive the problems of a new world. But the divisional manager gave me a promotion and transferred me to Gandhi Nagar. This was the city of films in Bengaluru. The office situated a little away from the Majestic Bus Station. I could learn the pulses of this locality with the hard work of four years.

Everything happened as expected. The transfer order came by courier. I saw a copy of the order in the morning itself. I made up my mind to leave this place. The next destination was a locality known as Gokulam in Mysuru. A farewell party in connection with this transfer was arranged with excitement by the colleagues. It was in an amusing manner that I accepted the transfer order. Without wasting time for further explanation, with my friend Vivi I bade goodbye to Bengaluru on 17 June.

# 2. Mysuru

VIVI, WHOSE real name is Viveesh, has been my friend since childhood. Both of us were hard workers. In the evenings after school time, we would walk along the narrow countryside. We were also fond of tasty dishes. Our ramblings would end up at some restaurants at Thottilpalam. The bucks that we gather from our homes on some false reasons would be spent on parotta and beef. By dusk, we would return along some other routes. New routes would also be discovered each time.

A lot of stories along the way. The beauty queens, teachers, child politicians, etc., would surface as characters of these stories. Firmly believing in two entirely different ideologies, we were unanimous in individual interests. It was after two years of my arrival that Vivi reached Bengaluru. As a revisit of the countryside meanderings, we put apart some time for wanderings here too on holidays.

I joined the office on June 17. I was well-received there. A good number of office staff members were from Kerala. Chitty collectors were from Karnataka. It might be because of my ability to speak Kannada, taught by the office attendant, people of this part spoke to me with admiration. Nevertheless, I had to start from scratch in Mysuru. Having strong confidence, which I got out of selling Eureka Forbes' vacuum cleaner from house to house, I took chitty tariff and set off to the shops in the city. I aimed to achieve success. I might get a transfer from here too. Still, I had to make my presence here.

I briefed the shopkeepers about the particulars of the chitty and gave visiting card to each. I met a Kannadite during one of such visits. His name was Sadasiva whose wife was from Kerala. It was, therefore, easy for me to introduce the chitty conducted by Sree Gokulam Chit & Finance Company. Giving them an enrolment form I left for another client. It was thus my daily routine to seek new clients for enrolling them to chitty. On the fourth day of taking charge in Mysuru, I visited the Axis Bank branch there to open a savings bank account. Here I met a new guy, Nuthan, a villager from Karnataka.

Majority of the people I met here were from a similar background. During our chat, we talked about chitty too. In a few minutes, I could win him over, clarifying his apprehension about chitty procedures. Thus, I brought him to such a situation where I could bring Nuthan's enrolment form. It seemed to me that the distance between the afternoon and evening was quite long. By five o'clock, I came back to the bank. Nuthan was not there. He asked me over the telephone to wait till the next morning. But I had to wait for four days before getting his signature in the enrolment form. That was the first successful enrolment in Mysuru though it took around eight days.

I came back to my office with an elated mind and felt proud of myself. I now have learned that it was not futile to visit business firms as well. Many people called me and I gave them the details of the chitty procedures. New members poured in; many of them came on the lookout for me. I will climb up the stairs of success here too. With more confidence, I returned to that dirty quarter of mine in Mysuru.

To my utter surprise again, another transfer order, that too to a place unexpected! My feet began to stagger when the once-abandoned ill habits returned. I slept on the lullabies of alcohol; wandered in the clumsy streets of Mysuru throughout the night. Now it seems to me that Bengaluru was heaven compared to Mysuru. However, I was able to adjust to this environment easily within a few days. I ate food from the makeshift restaurants of Mysuru, due to the technical issues relating to the shifting of gas connection from Bengaluru to Mysuru. Liquor made my nightlife more colourful. Dinner was also from the above-mentioned restaurants.

Struggling back to the apartment, I would buy groundnuts and cornflakes from street vendors. Fried river fish became an integral part of my food. Money didn't matter. The chitty amount saved from Kerala, the advance amount for the apartment I got back from Bengaluru, and lastly the salary for the month would amount to one lakh rupees in the bank account. The food habit I had learned from Bengaluru has started to tumble me down. Non-vegetarian food, from unhygienic street restaurants, became my habit. The taste was perfectly nice. In Bengaluru, quite contrary to here, I cooked on my own. Only on weekends and holidays did

I have food from outside. Everything got derailed here. No restrictions on food; no one to control me, and I couldn't control myself too.

Preparing a list of chitty defaulters, I left the office with Sudheer to meet the clients. We visited their homes apart from the houses of the guarantors too. It was threatening through outward smiles. When it was around three o'clock we couldn't control our appetite. Upon Sudheer's suggestion, we went to a Malayali mess. And ate lunch there sumptuously. Rice, fish curry, fish fry, crab fry and beef. The stomach was more than full and on leaving the restaurant we asked for the parcel of four bondas. We headed to Sudheer's house. The tiredness was over and we ate the bondas as a snack in the evening along with tea. However, my stomach began to feel restless. The food perhaps was not right to my stomach at this time. By evening, I began to feel stomach pain. I went down to the medical store. Got six pills from there. I didn't bother about the name of the medicine. The pharmacist had told me that it was a stopper.

Another day dawned after the usual night sights of Mysuru. July 20. Gathering more addresses, I was accompanied by Kannadite Ramesan in my search for customers for enrolment in chitty. As these visits were result-oriented, our efforts became more dynamic. Ramesan had a sense of responsibility. We could even reach the remote rural locales of Mysuru, in search of clients for chitty. By noon, there were signs of rain in the atmosphere. Even under the strong and heavy drops of cold rain, we commuted to the next dhaba.

We took the company of Yogesh who was the daily bill collector of that locale. Again a day of sumptuous food, north Indian style. Chicken fried rice, kebab, rumali roti, then bangada. Ripping through incessant rain, our two-wheeler ran towards the office. We couldn't enjoy the wonderful sights of rain as it was torrential. Closing the eyes tightly, I sat behind Ramesh clasping him around his stomach. Still, I was completely drenched in water. When I got into the office, the manager smiled dryly, I was certain that was not because of intimacy with me.

The body had an itching sensation, which might be due to my exposure to rain. This was followed by restlessness and exhaustion. Last night, I had taken the second stopper that brought the stomach ache to a perfect halt. My mind became empty on my return from work. Some thoughts of unknown pain would make it more restless. The pledges taken under the blankets every morning would go away with the wind. My bike would stop in front of some bars. I got some peace there. The waiter would fetch my usual brand with the same pattern of the smile. Sometimes I would think the source of mental peace and love is this addiction to liquor and spending time here. No one has sorrows, no complaints, only happiness. Then why do you argue against liquor? With a staggering body and stooping head, I finally reached my clumsy apartment.

My roommate advocate Krishna from another part of Karnataka had left for home. He was garrulous and would go on incessantly with his habit of talking about anything on earth. He belonged to a remote rural locale in Mysuru. Opening the window, I took the key kept on the windowsill. The right hand didn't feel well. Exhaustion was felt. So I used both hands to open the door and somehow entered the house.

It was my habit to have a shower at night, however late I reach home. When I completed wiping the body with the towel, I heard the telephone bell ringing. That was one of my elder sisters. Answering it I held it on my left shoulder and put on my clothes. She informed and invited me to her house warming. "Thinking of the first person to invite, your face came to my mind," she said. I felt more affection for her at that moment. We chatted continuously. The food parcel was uncovered then. Rice bath and two idlis.

Watching television, I finished dinner and returned to the broken old sofa. I used to sleep on it every day. The fan would be working throughout the day however cold it was. I was habituated to its crunchy noise that would cause me to sleep. I should get up very early tomorrow, it was the annual day of the chitty company. Setting the alarm at 4 o'clock on the mobile phone, I lied on the sofa staring at the ceiling fan.

Last year's annual celebration was quite pompous. We were the stars of the party. It was arranged at a three-star hotel at Majestic area in Bengaluru. In remembrance of the NSS activities during my undergraduate programme at CKGM College, Perambra my speech and folk songs had dominated the entire celebration. The company chairman was astonished when he watched the programmes.

"Wonderful!" he commented.

He didn't forget to appreciate and congratulate us. There were three categories of competitions and we won them all. I remember everything as if it happened yesterday.

Tomorrow was the next annual celebration. This time we have arranged a tour of GRS Fantasy Park, Mysuru. Suddenly the phone started ringing. It was my beloved friend. I told her some lies especially trying to hide from her the recently resumed drinking habit. We had a long chat, and I fell asleep slowly.

# 3. What happened to this man?

I COULDN'T remember when I fell asleep, talking about the next day's tour to my beloved. I heard the mobile alarm yelling out, reached the phone and turned off the snooze and tried to get out of my bed. I was quite happy.

However, I felt that I couldn't get out of bed. The body doesn't move. I tried again and again. No change. Putting both elbows as the support I tried to lift the body somehow. Hands too didn't move then. I was worried; what happened to me? Why couldn't I move? What happened to my hands? Still, consoling myself internally I continued my efforts to get up. I should get up because I had a trip that day, and that would give me the happiest moments in life, I thought.

Lying on one side, I slowly rolled down from the sofa and was able to get up with greater effort and thus felt relieved. Then, I could walk. It was when I tried to open the door, I recollected yesterday's problem. The door handle didn't work then. I opened the door now with more effort and stepped on to the street. Mysuru was fully awake now. Chilly outside. Having a cup of tea at the nearby bus bay, I returned to the apartment.

Still, my tiredness increased. Nothing else. I was unable to find out a reason for this state of fatigue.

At last, I called Vivi, pressing the phone to my ear.

It was four o'clock in the morning. He might not have got up yet. I usually disturbed him when there was something quite important to talk about. He would not just hear my words, but he would do whatever he could to help me. Yes, the phone was ringing on the other end. He picked up only towards the last ring. His words were sleepy. It was only then I remember that his office was on a holiday.

"What? What happened?" he asked.

I told him everything.

He said that he too would face such situations when he felt exhausted often, similar to the one happened to me. The body would turn numb if you sleep on the sofa. It would take a long time to be all right. On his instructions, I walked along the road for a long-distance and walked back. Though it was early morning, the streets were quite busy with people going to the market to sell their vegetables on carts. You could find children on their wheeled carts pulled by themselves. When the fatigue increased, I called Vivi again. As he listened to my wavering voice, he said:

"Don't worry, I will start now."

I thought of contacting home in Kerala. What should I tell them? But if I don't tell them?

My legs also showed symptoms of numbness. Later, I called my elder brother and told him what happened. He too was in a sleepy mood. I doubted if he muttered something.

After walking some more, I returned to my apartment. I took the key from the windowsill and tried to open the door. Thought that everything would be alright soon. Not possible to open the door. Used both hands to turn the key. The hands have lost their strength. The key broke. Attempted again. When this also failed, I sat on the doorsill for some time. I slowly walked to the shed opposite the apartment. It had been used as a car garage. The watchman of this area would usually come there to get water from the tap nearby. I told him everything in Kannada. He was busy preparing tea on a kerosene stove.

I didn't know which language he spoke. His name is Das Prakash, which I learned just then. He came to the apartment with me and calling the house owner auntie, he got another key and opened the room and went back. By this time, I had been in such a state in which I was not able to get up from my seat.

I called my brother again. I understood that they had started from Kerala. I want to have a shower. Wrapping the towel around my waist, I got into the bathroom staggeringly. Poured water all over the body. I felt quite relieved then. Applied soap all over my body and I had to wash away the foam. I tried to pick the mug up from the bucket. It slipped out of my hand. I bent down to take it up, but as the knees too bent, I fell on the floor under the tap.

The water was falling heavily on my face. I couldn't breathe. Death was near. I couldn't move my head away from the strong current of water. I couldn't turn off the tap too. Clinging firmly on the tap, I tried to get up with all my strength. Not possible. Then I crawled along the rough floor of the bathroom. The skin got hurt and severe pain on the wounds. The eyes had bulged out. I took a long deep breath again and again. I got my life back again! I was lying on the floor without my clothes on!

Again I crept and took out a cloth kept for washing in the bathroom and covered my body somehow. I started to call the auntie loudly. Neelamma was washing clothes under the water tap outside the apartment. She heard me crying and looked into the house. Seeing my situation, she went out of the house to bring auntie for help. Together with auntie, she tried to lift me. As the body was completely paralysed, they couldn't do anything. Neelamma was sent for Das Prakash. He came in, panting. So strong a man, he lifted me from the bathroom. I could stand. He wrapped the towel around my waist, bathed and wiped my body clean.

"Kachi elli?"

I was wondering. 'Kachi' in Kannada means 'underwear'.

Putting on jeans and a black shirt, Das sat me on a chair. Auntie brought tea and biscuit by now. Drank tea completely. It seemed the biscuits didn't go down my throat. I ate two biscuits with much effort. My brother phoned me asking about the route to this apartment. Vivi also was calling at the same time. I asked Vivi to go and bring them here and disconnected the call. Asking me to sit there, without moving, auntie, Das, and Neelamma left the room. This was a moment when I began to understand that the humanitarian aspect of living beings was not lost.

Neelamma was the beautiful servant of auntie's house. Her house was in a village in the district of Mysuru, a little away from the city. Her husband was an alcoholic. The livelihood was earned by Neelamma. She worked in other households too. She earned more than 20,000 rupees per month. She had promised that she would wash my clothes. For a month I should pay Rs. 300. She had been said to be a relative of Siddaramaiah, once the chief minister of Karnataka, belonging to the Kuruba community. I had read about Siddaramaiah as hailing from a poor family. Therefore, Neelamma had a small influence among those who knew her well. Those who came from different localities and communities gathered under one roof like this. I, house owner auntie, three children, Das Prakash, Advocate Krishna, etc. I was really surprised about their consideration for me as if they were my brothers, sisters and my mother.

A car reached in front of the apartment in a quarter of an hour. My brother was accompanied by my friend Linoop. Vivi brought them here. The driver also got out. He was quite young. Vivi held my hand and I slowly walked towards the car and got into it with much difficulty. Auntie and her children came out of the house. I was seeing her children for the first time. Usually, they wouldn't be seen outside. Neelamma was also asked to get into the car. She sat in the front and began to tell the route to a hospital she was familiar with. The young driver sped fast through the route as per her directions. We reached in front of the hospital. Its name was Vatsyayan Hospital.

Reading its name I got up from the seat and slowly moved towards the hospital. As viral fever was rampant at this time, the hospital was crowded with patients, but due to the timely intervention of Neelamma, we possessed an OP ticket without delay. I was sitting among other patients eagerly waiting for their turn to consult the doctor. No symptoms of disease outside and I was quite healthy in their eyes. Naturally, they began to surprisingly stare at me whispering among themselves in Kannada:

"What a man is he? Why can't he give respect to the elderly?"

They were talking about something else too.

Their wrath began to go up in double hearing my name called out instead of the OP ticket number. They were a little relieved only when they saw me being carried away by Linoop and Vivi from my seat as if in a stretcher. I enjoyed these scenes with a little amusement in mind.

In the examination room, I was laid on a bed. Two doctors started examining me with a small hammer. They asked me to submit a blood sample when they couldn't completely come around the cause of my ailment. Vivi and Linoop went out with the sample. He didn't accept money from me to pay the bill. Assuming that the prognosis and diagnosis would consume more time, Neelamma was sent back on an auto-rickshaw.

The doctor said: "If it is sodium deficiency, we can find a solution. You'll be okay by tomorrow. For those two days stay here is essential."

I spent time praying that let it be because of sodium deficiency. I phoned my colleagues who were on the excursion. None answered the phone. In the morning I had phoned Sudheer to say that my friends would be arriving, therefore it might not be possible to join them for the excursion. Why didn't he answer my phone? Was it because he was angry about my reply in the morning? After half an hour the blood test result was brought. As I am not ready to believe in fate, let me not mention it.

It was not the deficiency of sodium as I had desired. The doctor said: "You may go to a better hospital." Dr. Theju was a neurologist here. He said that there are good hospitals in Kozhikode city if we would like to go to Kerala.

The solitary life of about eight years in Bengaluru had fed me up. I had the desire of going home to take rest for some time. Nothing was certain about the condition of my present illness. On the advice of Dr. Theju, we decided to consult a doctor at Baby Memorial Hospital, Kozhikode. He gave us a reference letter to Dr. V.G. Pradeep Kumar. The car got back to my apartment once again. It was parked in the parking lot of Das Prakash.

My brother went to my room with Vivi to pack my belongings. I wanted to use the lavatory and indicated it to Linoop. He tried to support me to make me stand up. It was then I realised that my legs had become senseless.

As if cracking a joke I told Linoop, "My legs are gone, Linoop. Pick me up." He called Das for help. They supported me on their hands and led me to the lavatory.

By the time my brother and Vivi brought out the suitcases from my room, auntie and her daughters came near me.

Auntie spoke in Tamil: "Don't worry. Everything will be all right. Please come back here after you're cured."

I nodded with a smile. We started.

Das took my hand and said: "Take it easy. On reaching home, phone me."

His eyes had turned red. Neelamma and auntie's eyes welled with tears as if they had met me for many years now.

The car moved slowly. With a smile, I waved my hands towards them.

# 4. To Kerala

VIVI GOT down at Mysuru bus station and he caught a bus to Bengaluru. The car hovered through the streets of Mysuru. Appetite began to sprout inside me. The bananas and other fruits displayed on the other side of the road were smiling at me. I had only two biscuits that I ate for breakfast. I was sitting beside Linoop at the back seat telling tales of many types. The driver too joined our conversation at times. They told me about the obstacles on the road to Mysuru by wild bamboos lying across.

We stopped by at certain points on the way that looked quite solitary as well as beautiful. We could see small thatched sheds where sugarcane was churned into brown sugar blocks in big pots. We passed along big panoramic vineyards and extensive vegetable farms. The speed of the car has increased. I had some doubts about the young driver, but I didn't say anything. After half an hour, I got a call from Vivi. I had some difficulty in putting the phone to my ear.

The doctor suspected that the cause of my illness might be the toxic contents in my food. When I related the case of diarrhoea that happened two days ago and how I managed to get relief by using a stopper medicine, the doctor confirmed that it was true. My brother had been busy informing my house about my condition. I told Vivi that the gas connection should have to be brought to Mysuru on my arrival from the hospital.

"First, see how long you would have to spend at the hospital, then we will decide about the return."

I had exactly calculated the intensity of my disease, but I didn't want to exhibit it. This attitude of mine might be a genetic trend. I remembered one such fatal experience when I got discharged from the ICU of Sagar Hospital in Bengaluru two days after a surgical procedure on functional endoscopic sinus. While I was sleeping I felt something like liquid on my face. I got up startled and saw that blood was gushing forth from my mouth and nose alike.

On the clock, the time showed three in the morning. The washbasin was immersed in blood. Later I rode on my bike to meet the doctor and returned. Yet, when I recalled that experience, fear didn't have any role there too. We had already passed Gundalpet and our car started cruising the cool greenery of Wayanad district of Kerala. Four o'clock then, I had almost forgotten hunger. The car halted in front of a countryside village teashop.

As I was completely paralysed, both the feet motionless, I was manually carried to the shop. It was natural that rural folk would notice everything that happens around. Likewise, people were closely observing us. For me, bread was ordered. Others asked for something else. They dipped the bread into tea and put it in my mouth. I tried to take in. But it didn't go down.

Not possible at all. A small portion slowly went down somehow. I didn't tell them about this. I told them that I didn't want anything for snacks. I realised that the control of my body was slowly slipping away from me. Despite all, I was talking continuously without losing the balance of mind. I was again carried in their hands while getting out of the teashop. I saw some young men looking at me, and whispering among themselves and laughing. One of them raised a common doubt loudly:

"Aren't you from Mysuru? Completely booze?"

I knew that they made this witty remark without analysing the situation. Smilingly I told them that we were going to the hospital for emergency treatment. Hearing the reply, the smiles disappeared from their faces. Without waiting for an answer from them, the car moved fast.

It was at five o'clock. Phoned my mother.

"Don't you like to come to Bengaluru to look after me? I am planning to come there for some days. You can take care of me there!"

I presented everything as if I was narrating a humorous story. Then I phoned my uncle. I told him everything but left out the emergency I was going through. Disconnecting the phone, I held the left window by pressing hard. But the hand's power had lost.

Another shock. The left palm has turned immobile.

"Linoop, the left hand also is lost," I said with a smile.

I was trying to conceal the growing fear. The young driver looked at my face. He had recognised everything.

The car speed was 110 kph now. His foot pressed the accelerator constantly.

The front lights were on. The sun was about to go down in the west. The driver pressed the horn and the car was running fast. My notion about this young man was completely wrong. He was speeding it using hand signals, overtaking vehicles at times, and resorting to other techniques like a skilful ambulance driver. It was the month of fasting for Muslims and the people had gathered along the road in towns about the time to break the fast after sunset.

All were watching us because of the ear-breaking horn of the car too. Surprisingly enough, it was not possible to see anyone with displayed illness in the car. It was because of this that some of them were angry with us. After some time, one of the horns got damaged. The vehicle sped fast with the sound of one horn. It was pitch dark outside the car. It had passed at 8 o'clock. We reached Kozhikode city. The traffic policemen knew the emergency and facilitated our onward movement at traffic signals. Our car ran toward like a VIP vehicle. Pressing the horn constantly the driver took the car to the porch of Baby Memorial Hospital, Kozhikode.

# 5. Baby Memorial Hospital

MONI KISHORE, my brother-in-law, along with my uncle and some others were waiting to meet us at the hospital. By the time the car reached there, two men in the blue uniform, brought a stretcher immediately. My brother together with brother-in-law and Linoop lifted me and laid on the stretcher. Though every part of my body, except the right hand, was completely paralysed I lay on the stretcher with a smiling face. They took me to the consultation room. The junior doctors examined me. They also used the hammer-like instrument. The angels were busy taking samples of blood for laboratory and they were sending the results by and by. I couldn't measure the time. The hospital was busy with people wearing white, blue and rose coloured uniforms. As time went by, my eyesight was getting dimmed gradually. Was I moving to death, to an unconscious state, or a coma?

No idea.

I began to feel completely blank all over my mind and body as if a live show slowly dissolves into indefinite or infinite darkness. Linoop stood by my side with a half-smile. He pressed my hand displaying a unique intimacy. I also smiled at him; the smiles on the faces of my brother as well as my brother-in-law were fading.

The eyesight is getting blurred every moment. An angel came there with some reports. The chief physician read the result. The doctor and the angel said nothing. It was the moment when I felt mentally broken. The moment my mind had doubts about the possibility of returning to life again.

Vivi called me again. Linoop answered the phone and put it to my ear.

"Don't worry. It is not a food poison. Perhaps, the body will paralyse completely and then your strength will come back step by step. You'll come back to normal life."

I was always confident in him.

With his usual smile, he continued: "I browsed internet about the symptoms. And, I phoned some doctors too. There is nothing to worry about. Ninety-nine per cent of patients have recovered completely. Usually, this malady affects the body slowly and gradually. If diagnosed properly and treated well, the patient will recover completely. However, in your case, the illness started in one day and developed into a severe stage. This happens rarely. Still, there is nothing to worry. It will perhaps take some time to get completely cured."

I heard everything he uttered. I also realised the fact that I need not fear death. Vivi's words also gave me self-assurance and more strength. There was a hope of a return to life. I had no lost dreams. I had spent my childhood in full celebration. The adolescent period was enjoyed in full at CKGM College, Perambra. I had immersed in the most joyous period of life while I was in Bengaluru.

Now Vivi had been speaking with examples of recovery.

“So, did you recognise what the ailment is?” I asked him.

“Yes. It is called Guillain-Barre Syndrome.”

The hospital was crowded with people and the bustle and hurry seemed like that of a wedding party.

Again, I brought the phone closer to my ear. Was it said by Vivi or was it a voice unknown? The sound echoed in the entire hospital:

“Guillain-Barre Syndrome!”

# 6. ICU

THE DIAGNOSTIC tests and examinations were over. After proper prognosis and diagnosis, the doctors decided to provide me with the required treatment. Again, the stretcher began to roll on. Lifts were waiting for me. I lay on the stretcher in a state of semi-consciousness without knowing where and what for I was running along. I was taken from one room to another along the frozen allies of Baby Memorial Hospital.

In the end, it reached in front of a glass door. In the green dim light, I read the board on the top, Neuro ICU. Opening the door a few angels received me with smiling faces. The young men in blue uniform took the stretcher in. Some angels stepped on to the bed. Two of them remained on the floor. Along with the bedsheet, I was taken out of the stretcher as if a little child to lay slowly on the bed. Taking the sheet back from the bed, the stretcher men left the room with it. I heard some beep voices. As if in an advertisement, I knew some lines moving in and out. I kept my eyes closed as if in meditation.

It was cold. An angel covered me with a blanket. She asked my name and asked many other questions. Her name was Anu. I am referring to them as angels not without a reason. For the four months I spent in the hospital, they were truly angels to me. A few more angels came to acquaint with me. I gradually experienced that my ability to speak was getting diminished. It is not even possible to let in the saliva at the mouth. I lay there some time in this state. My vision and consciousness had strains again. I felt in the mouth the saliva getting clotted, not able to take in or spit out. With the right hand, paralysis came to cent per cent.

Only consciousness remains to leave me. Everything is revolving, and in the end, it culminates at one point. At this point, there is a sphere of light. There came a nurse and she switched on a machine that was installed on the right side of my bed. She took out a small pipe from its farther end and inserted into my throat. Its name was the suction tube.

The pain was unbearable. The sphere of light was getting enlarged in proportion to the increasing rotation. I felt that some liquid was being taken out through the suction tube. My mind told me that the rotation would stop after the entire liquid has been taken out. Eyes had already bulged out. The liquid didn't get exhausted even after repeated suctions. My body, mind, the angels and the hospital were rolling around. I feel that my mind was losing control over the body. Blood pressure had gone above 220 and reached its optimum level. Head seemed to explode. Angels were in a bustle.

The sphere of light got widened and spread over the entire hospital and at once disappeared. There was darkness everywhere. Silence had gripped the entire world around me. I had entered the decisive phase of my sickness. Yes, unconscious state or coma. No certainty about anything. For one day, I was lying almost dead. I didn't know what happened to me during this fatal phase of my unconsciousness. Nor did I ask anyone about it.

I began to get back my eyesight on the second day. By the time I got back the consciousness, I found myself in a ventilator, where I could realise that I was given oxygen. To keep the ventilation tube intact, it was fastened to my head. I couldn't open my mouth. The air was lashing against my chest.

A state of restlessness and immobility. Blood pressure was still high. My dress was changed and now I was wearing a dhoti and a t-shirt. Air-conditioner is functioning restlessly; still, I was sweating all over. Visitors had flowed in. In a semi vision, I could see my friends standing around the bed. They were all received with a smile. I couldn't recollect who exactly the visitors were. After their departure, new visitors arrived there, neighbours, friends, relatives, etc. They had brought with them the shadows of fear and fright. The angels kept on asking who they were.

I could recognise them all. At last, my brother, brother-in-law, and Linoop entered the room. Then I felt more relieved. Brother-in-law consoled me:

"Don't worry. Everything is okay now. We will wait outside the ICU."

I didn't ask about anyone.

"Visiting time is over."

The deafening voice of a woman echoed inside the ICU. The visage of a strict and rough woman. She approached my bed with a simple smile.

A womanly face, fearless steps, and her eyes give out a look of certainty. This was Sheena, the nurse in charge of Neuro ICU. She ordered everyone to leave the room.

"This is the time for doctors' rounds."

She came near my bed and asked me as if someone very intimate to me:

"Rasith, are you okay?"

My reply was a smile. She had located my name from the list of patients.

She continued:

"You are suffering from Guillain-Barre Syndrome and we will start treatment tonight. There will be a plasmapheresis for five days. Then your weariness and paralysis will gradually get down and you'll come back to a normal state."

The doctors came one by one for checking. First was my specialist Doctor V.G. Pradeep Kumar, who looked like a beautiful Bollywood villain. A smile on his face. Calling out the names of each patient from the list, they interact with them as if they knew them all personally. Sheena chechi didn't escort them. She was sitting in her cabin. They examine the unconscious patients by using the small torchlight that she carried while going for rounds. I couldn't make out why they used this technique of looking into their eyes. Following them, another doctor appeared whose name was Abdul Salam. He was the Head of the Department of Neurology.

Seeing him, Sheena chechi got up, greeted him in modesty and escorted him. VGP approached me. It may be since I was from Bengaluru, he asked me in Hindi:

Rasith bhai, kaisa hai?

I had the desire to say an answer, but the ventilator tube remained an obstacle. Therefore, my answer was confined to a smile.

"We can start treatment today. Don't worry, everything will be alright."

His words of finiteness enhanced my confidence and more than medicine, those words would inspire and help conquer my sickness.

"Let us remove this ventilation soon and almost half of your illness will be cured with this." The doctor continued.

His first words about the ventilator remained in my heart as a deeply unabated presence. I began to chew those words and therefore repeat them:

"Let us remove this ventilator first."

VGP departed after giving the required directions to the angels.

One more doctor appeared before me. His name was Ummer Karadan. A doctor with a serene face and a simple smile. He constantly maintained a low tone of voice. All the doctors left the ICU after their routine rounds of examination.

ICU remained calm always, with only one exception, that of the 'beep' sound and Sheena chechi's voice as if a constantly heavy rain had come to a complete halt this time.

"Hey, children, care the patients well," Sheena gave instructions to the angels.

I noticed some student nurses entering the room with closed tiffins in their hands. What were these containers comprised of?

Perhaps, some food items.

I started salivating about its thought.

They walked to the right corner of the room; my eyes also moved along with them. Since I am staying put in the room, I am compelled to adapt to the situation somehow. Observation of the happenings in the room is the only solution I have in hand now. My observations included the movements and chats of other patients, the nurses, the bystanders, the sweepers who went on cleaning the room as well as the veranda with their vacuum cleaners.

The student angels opened their containers. There were cotton clothes and plasters.

I saw them sorting and arranging them in order on a tray. They were talking to Sheena chechi and laughing intermittently. Sheena chechi also noticed it. Her eyes could scan each and everything in the ICU at a glance.

Sticking her eyes on to the floor, without paying attention to anything, she commanded,

"Come on, lass, we have got a lot of work."

Though I had forgotten my sense of appetite, I started to feel tired.

I was asking a question to myself: "How can I take food?"

Just a minute was over when Sheena chechi came to my side with a small plastic cover. Opening the bag, she said:

"Rasith, this is Ryles tube. You can't consume food now. That means you can't orally take in food. So we will provide food through this tube for some days."

With those words, she began to insert the tube through my nose. The nasogastric tube was usually passed through the nose into the stomach. Due to suffocation, I began to cough continuously.

"Take in saliva well, then you won't have a cough."

I did as she instructed. I could experience the tube getting down through the glottis into my stomach. The tube was plastered well over my nose. Checking whether the tube was well inserted, and confirming it Sheena chechi instructed the assistant to pour in food in liquid form into the tube and left. I didn't feel much difficulty after the tube was inserted.

I could see the semiconscious patients who were the inmates of my ward, disconnecting the tubes without being noticed by the angels. Perhaps, it was with the awareness that to survive me Ryles tube was necessary that I didn't attempt to take it out or it might be because I began to develop a liking for the same. I didn't take it seriously though it was quite disturbing.

Another angel came there. She looked short, and with smiles, she asked my name. Then she started feeding me casually and engaging me in a soft talk, though I was unable to make out what she was reaching for. I watched her curiously. Removing the cap of the tube, she inserted the small end of the big syringe to pump in water at first. Knowing that the water was entering my stomach, I felt a cool comfort.

As the feed brought in the morning had turned stale, a fresh feed had been arranged. It also began to go down the tube slowly. While it was flowing down, my eyes also began to go down the tube slowly along. It was then I noticed the small angel's name, Chinchu Chacko, inscribed on her identity tag, hanging from her neck.

She asked: "Hey, did you get my name?"

I nodded.

After pouring porridge, she poured in the water again and took out the syringe before recapping the tube. She took the syringe for clearing. Returned and asked if I was happy. She inquired about my life and I realised that poor Chinju didn't know anything about my life.

She left me to attend another patient. It was her turn to attend me that day. I resumed my surveillance. The angels were busy giving all sorts of care to the patients in the unit. Their duties included giving medicine, injections, drips, moving them on one side, putting blankets on, etc.

They also took care of the Ryles tubes and was vigilant if these tubes were removed by them. They received new patients and gave them first aid before taking them to their respective beds. I had seen the patients being treated from their trolleys by these nurses. They were always active and never seen relaxing. They took care of everything and were always smiling.

I even thought if the angels were more attentive than the doctors. May not be so because the diagnosis of a patient is the primary step in treatment. Otherwise, why wasn't it possible for the doctors in Mysuru Vaatsalya Hospital to diagnose my disease? Physicians prognose and diagnose the illness and prescribe the proper treatment. The angels care and please the patients in addition to obeying and implementing the orders of the doctors.

# 7. The angels of BMH

I COULDN'T measure time even after the second feeding was over. It was around two o'clock in the afternoon. I spotted the angels of the next shift entering the ward carrying their bags. They took pen and paper to note down important assignments of the nurses of the morning shift. So they had to go to the patients and naturally they approached me too. I felt that they were looking at me in surprise.

After they left the room, Chinchu Chacko came to me and said:

"Brother, my duty is over; I'm going. It was the duty shift that you've just seen. Let's meet tomorrow."

She pressed my inactive hand. What modesty! Treating patients as if at one's own home! Were they the ones not well taken care of by our society? They were not nurses, but they are the real angels. The angels were wearing white clothes and smiling. They came to look after me only, I thought.

In the evening duty, it was Steffi, who attended me. I was a 'case' for them. The case is the hospital name for patients in our country. But I didn't want to be known by this label. Steffi talked with a half-smile and she had a tone of affection to all. Steffi also asked the routine question. But she was a little faster in her talk. The way of her talk was comfortable to my ears. Everyone behaved with a pleasant visage to me.

I was perhaps the only conscious patient in the unit now. At five o'clock Sheena chechi finished her duty. Next feed was also over. It was at six o'clock. Steffi came and inserted a cannula on my left hand. She explained that it is meant for administering injections at times. It was quite painful but I didn't express it. It was only a beginning. Since then, I didn't remember how many injections were done on my body. The total of injections and piercing the body to find nerves would come to approximately above 300.

Steffi hung the bottle of medicine on the hanger of a stand and took the tube in hand to insert into the cannula opening its top. Turning the knob on the tube to the right the sparkling liquid began to flow into my nerves. Then, on instructions from the doctors, pills were pounded with a pestle in a small mortar and mixed with water to pour into the Ryles tube. I lay on the bed looking at the drip-drop of the medicine.

Steffi walked over to another patient asking me to tell her when the medicine gets exhausted. Seven o'clock. I saw a woman attendant bringing tea and snacks upon the order of these angels. By then, all angels gathered together removing their gloves washing their faces and hands. They poured in tea into the glasses and enjoyed the ethnic snacks I observed with interest. I didn't feel salivating. When could I take those snacks again? When they noticed that I was seen watching them, they moved to their nursing cabin to have tea.

By the time they finished tea, the medicine in the hanging bottle was over. Steffi came and removed the empty bottle and deposited it in the box kept in the corner of the ICU. I was salivating continuously. The angels had a tough time using the suction tube to take out saliva. Some announcements could be heard often. It was at nine o'clock. The angels for the night shift also arrived one by one.

The same shifting ceremony. The same system of note-taking (scribbling on notepads). I observed the new angels. Apart from them, there was a male angel too. When they were passing in front of me, I read his name from the tag: Haris. A childish face, an almost the same kind of smile. I watched the angels of previous shift moving out of the hospital. The nurse in charge of me during the night shift was Betty, who was a senior member. She was vibrant and loud-voiced. It could be read from her words that she was a senior nurse. She started her duty.

It seemed time was moving quickly. A man dressed in a white uniform accompanied by a beautiful assistant brought a huge machine rolling to my bedside. A big machine with a lot of small tubes, a stand and a monitor. Betty approached me and said, "Rasith, your first plasmapheresis will start now." Now I understand this machine was meant for that.

She continued: "Plasmapheresis is almost similar to dialysis. The liquid plasma will be replaced from the blood and taken out using this machine and new plasma will be infused into the body simultaneously."

I wanted to ask why it was done to me, but suddenly they located an artery on my thigh and penetrated with a needle. I had severe pain. Just a little away another needle too. It didn't give me pain, maybe because of the anaesthesia administered earlier. Still, I realised the truth that a device penetrated my flesh. Two tubes from the machine had been connected to the previous needles. With the dexterity of a magician, the man started pressing the bottom on the machine. He had been carefully watching me, but I couldn't make out his facial expressions as he was wearing a mask.

At last, after pressing a button, the white tubes began to turn red. My warm blood began to flow into the machine through one tube. By travelling through the unknown areas of the machine, it reached another tube. The plasma, which had been in the hanging bottle, began to slowly enter the blood, thus filtered. The blood and the new plasma joined together, started entering my body through the syringe inserted on the other part of my thigh. It was one o'clock after midnight. As if in a dream in half asleep, I lay on the bed looking at the process of plasmapheresis.

The time was beyond two o'clock. Plasmapheresis was over. Turning off the machine completely they took out the syringes from my thigh. The influence of anaesthesia lessened. The attendants pulled the machine out from the ICU. Betty put my dress in order and covered me with a blanket. Even without blankets, I was sweating, though it was in an air-conditioned room.

Betty returned to her seat in the nursing room asking me to sleep. I saw others walking around like watchmen. Some patients were trying to remove their Ryles tubes, but the attempts were foiled due to my observation. Sleep has abandoned me, and I was in an insane situation. I tried again and again to sleep but it was in vain. Therefore, I was in a helpless condition. More than those who observed me, it seemed that I was observing them as if they were my case.

Time is 3.30 in the morning. Betty and others started clearing the patients one by one. They were busy putting on new dresses after wiping their body with towels and changing their blankets and bedsheets. In half an hour, Betty and Bijina came to my side.

“Rasith, let us have a bath, sponge bath,” said Betty.

She took out a fragrant wet paper named Easy Bath and began to wipe my face. Though it was quite chilly, I felt more comfortable and tended to sleep. It was at 5 o’clock, the sponge bath was over for all the patients. Slowly sleep overtook me. In sleep, I could feel something piercing my body. Suddenly, I woke up and saw that Bijina was searching for a vein on my hand to take out a blood sample. Since then, I lost my sleep throughout the day. I lay on the bed looking at the window through which sunlight was entering the room at a slow pace.

The next work shift was at 7.00 am. Chinju Chacko came to the room with a broad smile. The baton of the next duty had been handed over by Betty and others. Chinju kept her bag at the nursing room and approached me. After the routine greetings and hellos, she started suction. Another angel too came and they lay me on one side; applying some ointment on my back, they began to beat with their hands. When the beating crossed its limits, I stared at Chinju.

She said: "This is back care. If you lie on the bed like this, there is a chance for the skin to get blistered. It is to protect you from that we are doing back care."

I waited for the clock's hour hand to reach 7.30 am, because it was then the visitors were usually permitted inside the unit. They came one by one. My mother, sister, and brother-in-law got in at first. They talked to me with smiling faces. However, I could read their fear in their eyes. I was interested in talking about some other things. After they left some neighbours came. Their enquiries about my illness disturbed me. I lay with my eyes closed, paying no attention to their words. Chinju asked me if I did not know them. I nodded with my head. Again some more visitors. I was afraid of looking at their frightened faces. Still, I spoke to some others.

The loud reminder of Sheena chechi: "Time over."

The day started with the doctors coming in for a routine check-up. VGP headed straight to me asking in Hindi: "Rasith bhai, kaisa hai?"

He took my photo and showed it to me. I felt a relief when I knew that my face hasn't got much change. He prescribed some medicines and injections.

"Keep Rasith in CPAP."

He then turned towards other patients. I looked at Chinju as if asking a question about what the doctor instructed.

She told me with a smile: "There are three modes in the case of a ventilator. For a patient who is unable to breathe, CMV mode provides full-time oxygen; only half of the help is given in the SIMV mode. The last mode is CPAP. In this mode, though the ventilator support is available, oxygen must be taken by the patient. So we are going to keep you in CPAP mode. This is another step for removing the ventilator."

A little scared though inside, I recalled the words of VGP, "Rasith, we should avoid this ventilator, then half of your illness will be over."

There was nothing else to think over and worry. I became more confident as I knew that a new dawn is waiting for me.

I saw Chinju pressing on some buttons meticulously with the skill of an expert. The air that was pumping into my chest stopped.

"Rasith, you breathe in the air well," Sheena chechi said. I felt as if taking charge of a new job. It was today that I understood breathing was a heavy burden.

I had to take in breath continuously with a balanced speed; a little carelessness would invite loud alarm from the monitor. On hearing this, blood pressure will go up. I was keener on this new job. I look at the monitor at the interval. I always tried to keep an angel with me on the side of my bed. Therefore, I felt increased self-confidence.

Since then, I adopted several strategies to keep at least one of them always on my side. I would ask them to move my legs, wipe my face, mobilize my hands, etc. Even a moment without their company made my paralysed body more restless. It seemed that the angels were scolded by the management for remaining with me all the time. I could not observe through the ICU that day. Noting each movement of the breathing process intensely, I spent my time as if in meditation.

It was late evening. But I hadn't noticed the passage of time. The angels came and went, fed me, did the suction, beat on my back, doctors did the procedures, new patients got into the unit, deaths, relatives' cry, and prayer. Nothing could be observed. The entire time was spent on my breath, its ups and downs, and the alarm of the monitor. By the time it was evening, I could adapt to CPAP. Then I resumed my observation.

The discussion that day was mainly about the opening of the critical care unit. Here also we could listen to the pros and cons. They made references about a doctor named Anoop, who was supposed to be in charge of the unit. My mind also participated in the discussion silently, forgetting about CPAP.

Night arrived, which I didn't notice. The same young man and a lady in the same uniform came to the room to perform plasmapheresis. Everything was going on like yesterday. A little sedation. But when plasmapheresis reached halfway, some reactions began to happen on my body. Itching and a little discolouration on my body. The process for the day seemed to have finished soon.

Betty was in charge of the process as before. She behaved as if she was my guardian. My brother would phone her to inquire about my condition. I tried to keep her in my company.

After I was admitted in this hospital, I hadn't had a chance to sleep except falling into unconscious due to hypertension.

Apart from the routine scenes, which I witness every day in the ICU, I happened to witness anxiously the sight of a dying man. He was quite young. Married. I heard that he was an alcoholic. His liver had completely ruined. I lay constantly looking at his face. He was sweltering in the bed as if something was ripping apart his stomach sharply. He felt suffocated. Blood oozed out through his mouth and nose. The nurses were wiping his face. He looked sympathetically at the nurses and doctors.

Pressing on his chest, they administered CPR. Writhing and writhing in pain, eyes bulged out, sweating all over. Suddenly, he lay still with his body curved like a bow and legs stretched out. The monitor of the ventilator sounded the alarm. The duty doctor at night, Vineeta, confirmed his death, by checking with equipment.

It was the clarification of a doubt I had while I was in a bar at Mysuru. I found the answer to the question: "Why does society oppose alcohol?" in the screaming wife and child of this man. I lay observing the posthumous rites of the young man, led by Betty.

When she saw that I had been watching everything, she drew the curtain in front of me. I didn't notice the chilly sponge bath on the dead body. Morning dawned outside the ICU. With the eyes reddened due to excessive weeping, his wife and relatives went out after signing some important documents, following the dead body. One of the relatives could be heard talking over the phone about the arrangements of the funeral.

The routine visitors were not less on this day too. The gathering of my relatives at this hospital, though they were withered for various reasons, was a wonderful sight.

# 8. Life breath

VGP CAME for his rounds very early. It was always so. He photographed my face on his mobile phone once again. The face looked more tired. The eyes were quite exhausted due to sleeplessness.

VGP asked Chinju: "Aha, Rasith has improved a lot now. Today we can shift him to TPS."

He asked them to examine my chest, and send for X-ray. When he went out, I asked Chinju about TPS. Let me remind you that this is not Chinju Chacko, but Chinju Sunny, a fair and slim angel.

She said, "It is not TPS but T-Piece." It is the last step before completely removing the service of a ventilator. After disconnecting the ventilator tube, Chinju connected the T-Piece to another part of the ventilator, joined to the knob kept in my mouth and switched on. There was no change. I was losing breath. My eyes bulged out and I began to sweat all over. Monitor sounded the alarm loudly. Chinju was frightened.

Sheena chechi raised her voice and said:

"Rasith, take in breath well."

It was more difficult to breathe in with T-Piece than yesterday's CPAP. It was like pulling in some heavy gas from an unknown cave. I completely forgot ICU. Concentration was on only one thing. Still, I couldn't. I took a breath in gathering all my strength. Meanwhile, my blood pressure went up. I was getting more worried by the constant alarm of the monitor. Chinju was asked to stand by throughout. I asked her to move my hands and legs when BP seemed to be going up. And when Sheena chechi saw that I was improving, she asked a nurse to stay with me, giving me better relief.

My experience with T-Piece was more mechanical than that of yesterday. I didn't even notice when I was given food through Ryle's tube. I looked at the monitor constantly. Bijina came for evening duty. It seemed that I was getting appreciated by others for being in T-Piece. But I thought my breath would stop at any moment. The suction method of some angels was quite painful. They did the suction by inserting a long sharp plastic tube into my throat. They did this as if they were doing it to the patients lying unconsciously. I lay silently thinking about the celebration of a return.

Calculating the ups and downs of my breathing myself, I inhaled oxygen without knowing the passage of time. It was another guy who came for the third plasmapheresis that night. It began a little early. None of the problems like the previous day happened. But as the night was advancing, I began to feel tired due to the incessant breathing in and out. It was a great relief when Chinju Chacko was on duty at night. She spent her time with me until morning. She shook my hands and legs when I was afraid of rising blood pressure level.

She wiped my face with Easy Bath. She did suction whenever I asked her. I grew mad being sleepless at night. I failed in my attempt to sleep. After sponge bath Chinju made me lie on one side. There was one more attempt to fall asleep. My bed would always be with full of pillows. One was for the head, one for the legs, two for the hands, one as a support when I lie on one side. Pressing my face to the pillow once again, I tried to sleep, but I lay sweating on the bed. It was time again for the visitors.

"Brother, see who are here, your friends."

I was not in a mental condition to see anyone. Still, I opened my red swollen eyes slowly. Chinju laid me in the upward position. My friends from the native village were standing before me as though they were some shadows. I could only see Ajesh. I couldn't smile my usual smile. Eyes and their sight seemed to be heavy. Ajesh was shocked to see my exhausted and hard situation, with my eyes bulged and body sweating. The situation seemed to be getting worse owing to the fear that my BP would rise at any moment. I asked Ajesh with my eyes to leave the room. Judging the state of my mind, he took others with him towards the door. A relief when Chinju wiped the face with Easy Bath.

Vipi came to visit me that day availing a day's leave. One of my friends from Bengaluru also came with him. My eyes started sparkling with happiness when I saw him. They approached me with a broad smile. I tried to smile. Like before, he explained all aspects of my disease as well as the various stages of recovery with examples. My confidence shot up instantly.

After Chinju Chacko left, next morning Chinju Sunny came back. Senior in-charge was Betty in the morning. She too took care of me very much. I had a suspicion that Betty had a little haste to remove my ventilator. But when VGP came the next day, he instructed them to keep me in the same position one more day. It was then my first X-ray was taken. The members of the staff in blue uniform brought pushing along a big machine positioned in such a way to have the light on my chest. A board that seemed like a sheet was kept on the bed and put me over it.

Chinju said it was an X-ray cassette. My backside began to ache. The X-ray technician wore a special protective dress and instructed another to start the machine. The angels and other members of the staff present there ran away to safer places for cover from radiation. I was silently recreating the mischievous childhood days of the past when we played hide and seek. The power was on in the machine. The structure of my chest was filmed by the X-ray machine. In four and a half months, X-ray light passed through my body not less than fifty times. I saw the angels returning in a jovial mood. I wanted to tell them to remove the X-ray cassette, but I was unable to do so. I was writhing in pain. It took some more time before getting it removed from the bed.

Betty told me: "Rasith, this ventilator will be removed tomorrow."

Though I felt happy on hearing this news, I was doubtful if it would be possible to breathe myself.

# 9. Tracheostomy

I THOUGHT that only three or four days had passed after I came to the hospital.

Chinju said, “Today is August 1. It has been twelve days since Rasith came here.”

I was astonished. Ventilator had to be removed soon. Otherwise, I would have to go to the tracheostomy. It was the first time that I heard the word tracheostomy. Chinju couldn’t answer any questions clearly when I asked her about it. Though there were fluctuations in my BP, I was able to adjust with T-Piece. I resumed my observation. That day was the inauguration of the critical care unit, which had been the point of discussion in the nursing centre for long.

Dr. Anoop Kumar had already joined the hospital. He was about to visit the ICU. It was said that he had many years of experience in Aster MIMS Hospital, Kozhikode as in charge of the critical care unit. Though they were talking indolently about him, I could also read a curiosity in the eyes of hospital staff. I also wanted to see him because I had begun to dream about him as a hero and anti-hero. After some time, I saw a young man in a splendid dress, with an air of simplicity, pushing the glass door open and entering the room.

He inspected each of the ventilators minutely, and met the nurses in charge of each patient and instructed them on the course of treatment to be imparted. His way of the talk was polite and knowledgeable. He seemed to be not so friendly to others. However, he was meticulous in caring for the patients. I noticed him alerting the angels on all aspects of using ventilators. I remember one of such incidents in which he was too much strict on some matters. Ambili was a nurse at ICU. She was asked to remove the ring that she had been wearing on one hand. This was an occasion for other nurses to understand this gentleman as if through a microscope.

Chinju whispered to me: "The Critical Care Unit Head, Anoop sir."

When he reached near my bed, Chinju explained my case to him.

All the angels gathered around him in attention. Sheena chechi was also there, and that too, in front of them all. The doctor stepped out of the room after instructing the angels on various matters in his natural and stable voice. The nurses went to their cabin, keeping Dr. Anoop in the centre of their discussion. Closely observing Dr. Anoop's arrival, his procedures and return, the time had been flying.

My BP fluctuated at times; sometimes going up and sometimes going down. Ever since I was on T-Piece, suction had been done at times. I always forgot the fact that I was in an ICU. It seemed we were gathered in a hall for some rituals. It was like the hall of a big hotel, and the angels seemed to be workers.

Once I had met with an accident, and I was covered in a pool of blood. Even when my eyes were open, I felt that it was happening really. Frightened to the core of my existence, I asked the angels to hold me tightly. How could I disclose these feelings to them? Even now, the picture of that hotel remains with me.

Chinju Chacko came at night and woke me up. She asked me: "Chetta, are you dreaming?"

"This is your fifth plasmapheresis. After some days things will change. Tomorrow, after extubation is over, everything will be easier."

Extubation has been defined to me as removing the ventilator, while intubation was said to be putting a patient on a ventilator. The same technicians came for plasmapheresis this time too. I was happy; with usual anaesthesia, they started plasmapheresis.

Thus the last plasmapheresis was over. That night also I asked Chinju Chacko to remain with me. I took a breath in through the T-Piece. I felt tired once again.

She consoled me: "Everything will be alright, Rasith after extubation is over tomorrow."

I didn't know the real chill of a sponge bath. And it was morning.

VGP was accompanied by Betty.

"Rasith, shall we remove the ventilator?"

However, I felt that I was not confident about taking in breath myself without external help.

"No problem, sir. We can remove; there has been no problem with T-Piece for the last two days," said Betty with excitement.

Sheena chechi also reached there. They started to remove the ventilator. It was turned off at first. Breath stopped. I started to take in breath in with utmost effort. It was quite a heavy task. When I was not able to get enough oxygen, I moved my head sideways.

"Rasith, don't panic, take a breath in."

They thought that it was out of fear that I was unable to breathe well. It irritated me a little.

It was a fine discovery. My inability to breathe and wriggling oneself was out of fear!

Betty loosened the tie around my neck. She began to take out the tube and pulled out the knob. It was a lengthy one. I was really surprised to know that such a long tube was inserted into my throat. I saw Betty expressing her triumph by pulling out the tube slowly and looking at others.

Since my BP was steadily going up, Sheena chechi put the nebulisation mask on my face. She switched on the nebulizer.

"Take in breath well," Sheena chechi screamed.

It seems my vision is blurring. I started to throw my head on both sides. They couldn't locate a vein on my hands to take a sample of blood for examination. They inserted the syringe three times on my leg. But if I had been able to move my leg, Betty would have got a slap with it because I was suffering such severe pain. In my semi-consciousness, I looked at the people around me in despair. The syringes in Sheena chechi's hands looked like gigantic weapons. The people around me looked to be laughing at me.

At sight, the face of Dr. Anoop. He tapped at my shoulder and said:

"Tell me your name ... Tell me your name ..."

He asked my name two or three times. Even with the utmost effort, I couldn't tell my name. I was exhausted, breathing in.

"It is not the right time for the ventilator to be removed from him. He can't even move his tongue." I heard him saying.

It seemed that none paid attention to his words of expertise. BP shot up to the optimum level. I was between the devil and the deep sea. On one side, someone was trying to find a vein to take the sample of blood, and on the other suction was going on. My body was trembling all over. No breath. ICU was revolving.

After constant rotation, it became a little globe. There was a light. It grew bigger and bigger and filled the entire ICU and stopped suddenly. Darkness everywhere. Again, I was speeding and falling into unconsciousness.

## 10. In ventilator again

MORE THAN four hours had passed before I regained consciousness. I was put back on the ventilator again. There was a shadow of pallor on Betty's face. It was as if I had done some sort of a crime. Soon came ward secretary Sonia chechi's advice. Though it was out of love for me, it aroused a little anger in me. I tried my best but failed in controlling myself in this context. I was mentally broken.

Later I became a case of Nancy Binu. She loved and cared for me as if I was her brother. Realising my mental state she stood by me and assisted in regaining my confidence gradually. The tiredness after hypertension gradually decreased. Nancy talked to me. She was quite a rural person.

"Today we are going to do tracheostomy on Rasith. It is not advisable to keep ventilator through the mouth. There is every chance of infection. Instead of this, a small incision will be done on my trachea and then ventilator will be inserted there. This is tracheostomy," Nancy said.

I began to develop hypertension once again. I stared at Nancy.

"Don't get panic. This is a simple and small process. This will be done on anaesthesia. You will feel relieved after this tube is removed from your mouth," she consoled me with a smile.

Nancy was a smart girl who tried to complete the duties as speedily as possible. Therefore, I noticed that some odd things would happen in the ICU. She would be blinking at Sheena chechi's admonition at times.

I was not given food since this afternoon. A little tired. Before going to the operation theatre, food should not be taken in.

I waited for a long time. At last, at about 11 o'clock my dress was changed and I got a blue jubba (a long loose thin dress) which was the uniform for patients. The trolley arrived along with them. Ventilator tube was removed. The angels picked me from the bed with its sheets and lay on the trolley. It seemed my weight was lost a little. I gestured with the head that I was breathless. The ventilator on the trolley was connected to the knob on my mouth and it was turned on. Trolley moved out of the ICU slowly while Nancy followed us with the relevant medical files. I heard Sheena chechi announcing something through the microphone. So the path of my trolley towards the lift was empty. Some faces were waiting to see me. So I felt a little happy on this occasion. Brother, brother-in-law, uncle, Vivi's father, and more... My uncle came to my side and consoled me.

The trolley got into the lift and it went down. The security women in the lift looked and smiled at me indifferently. When the lift reached the floor where the operation theatre was situated, I saw that the pathway until the door of OT was evacuated by the security men as if they were waiting for a VIP. I was shifted to the OT table. Trolley ventilator was also removed and replaced by the OT ventilator. I realised that it was Dr. Praveen who would do the surgery. There were two lady assistants too.

"Rasith, you are going to get anaesthesia," Dr. Praveen said.

One of the assistants opened the cannula, and a drug was injected into it. I looked up. Five balls of light were shining from above. I felt something was rushing up through my blood. The light of the bulbs gradually dimmed. Voices got thinned and slowly disappeared. Lights dissolved into darkness. To unconsciousness at last.

I had to wait at the post-operative ward for two hours before getting shifted to the ICU on a trolley. My immediate thought was to reach somehow there. Postoperative ward was a strange place as far as I was concerned. Trolley had been brought afternoon. I hadn't completely regained consciousness. I hadn't wholly figured out about what happened around me.

While lifting me on to the trolley I could see that the ventilator knob was connected to my neck. Ventilator had been removed from my mouth. It was exhilarating as if a heavyweight had been taken out of me. The trolley finally reached the ICU. Shifting me to the bed, the ventilator was connected to tracheotomy and switched on. Half of my sickness seemed to be over now.

My uncle approached me.

"How do you feel, my boy?" he asked.

I could see that he had read my happiness easily. I could talk to him in a mild tone.

At very early morning, Nancy came to my side. I liked her frankness in talking. It was the first time after my arrival there that a person had a conversation about my personal life. Her sincerity impressed me. I told her about my life starting from CKGM College, Perambra until the time I fell sick in the short span of two hours.

She listened to my story as if it was an unbelievable riddle. The truth, though having a goal of success in life, failure defeated me, could invite sympathy in her. Since then she stayed with me to nurse and care. It was obvious that she gave more care to me than to others.

"We'll have to remove the ventilator. Forget the past. Rasith will come back to normal life. We should be able to prove to everyone that you can walk like others." Nancy's words energised me.

"Should come back, should come back" – my mind whispered repeatedly with more force and agility. Nancy's nursing gave me more confidence. After the next day's sponge bath, I had been shifted to CPAP.

Visitors' time. My visitors were restricted to the nearest relatives. They entered the room. I remembered Vivi's words: "Don't be angry with anyone." Still, if hypertension increases, my mental control would lose. Apart from my brother, Linoop was waiting outside the ICU. He was the first to reach the ICU. Last night his mobile phone was stolen while he was sleeping after a hectic day of fatigue. Though he narrated it like a funny story, it couldn't be read from his face. By then, my brother also entered the ICU. I noticed in his hand something looked like a fruit container.

It was an FM radio that had later undermined the silence and sorrowful atmosphere of this ICU during my stay. At first, I listened to the FM radio over earphone and later earphone was avoided, and I slowly increased the volume. Soon ICU was quite noisy with Red FM, Radio Mango, etc. It was a great relief to the angels too. I thought radio was more than a medium of enjoyment to them too.

Nevertheless, it became my pulse. There was a time when my brother had to be called through an emergency microphone to tune the channel. CPAP was not a problem for me. I didn't notice the passage of time due to the presence of the radio, my blood pressure remained the same. The feeding of juice through Ryles tube was not able to sustain my normal health. My bodyweight had been 80 kg when I was admitted here. Now, you could see that I had been reduced into a skeleton. I could see the daily changes through VGP's mobile phone. However, my hopes and confidence took me up to the sky.

VGP came for the rounds.

"Rasith bhai, kaisa hai?"

"Teek hum mein," my voice slowly rose evoking laughter in the witnesses.

I also laughed.

"Do you know how long you have been in the hospital?"

I thought I had been there for the last 12-13 days. But I was astonished to hear that it was 35 days since I was admitted at the hospital.

A man who didn't waste even a moment in life had been in the hospital bed for 35 days! VGP left the room instructing Nancy to replace the Ryles tube, otherwise, I would get infected. By the time VGP left Nancy came with a new Ryles tube. She slowly removed the old one and I could feel the tube moving slowly out of the bottom of my stomach. It had turned yellow.

I had a relief when it was removed from my nose. Earlier it was through the left nose that the tube was inserted; now Steffi unwrapped the new tube and began to insert it through the right nose. I got irritated. Steffi tried again and my BP shot up, leaving me unconscious instantly though I regained consciousness soon. When Steffi brought another tube, I signalled her not to insert it. Then came Sheena chechi. She also tried twice. The tube came out through my mouth making me cough heavily. Dr. Anoop came to the ICU to examine ventilator patients. Sheena chechi called him. He inserted the tube in a matter of seconds. No cough, no pain.

"During the insertion of the tube in the case of tracheostomy patients, you should deflate cough." He advised everyone. Steffi's face got pale, but Sheena chechi was happy to learn a new technique.

On August 26, 2013, VGP came to the ICU in the morning and directed them to do an X-ray on my chest after the examination was over. The blue uniform fellows came again to take my chest X-ray. Immediately after the X-ray procedures were over, I saw a charming young lady who wore a uniform similar to that of a doctor inquiring about me. I tried to listen secretly to her conversation with Nancy.

"His chest has got a small fracture, VGP asked me to do the therapy."

Nancy escorted her to my side.

"Rasith, from today your chest therapy begins, it will be helpful to remove the ventilator," Nancy informed me.

But she didn't mention the injury on my chest. They moved me to T-Piece from CPAP and began to tap on my chest after spreading a cloth. I was a little frightened at first due to the possibility of increased hypertension. I was getting suction after some time. The saliva had come down on the chest and congested there. I could see the yellow fluid flowing through the tube. Slowly, I noticed the power of tapping on the chest increasing. And the pain too was worsening. Still, it was relieving to see that my breathing got more ease gradually. The therapy continued for half an hour.

I asked Nancy after the therapist had gone out:

"When will they return to hit me?" I asked her jokingly. My question made her laugh.

"She will be back in the evening once again to hit you. Don't you want to get cured soon?" she replied with a smile. After the therapy was over, T-piece no longer became a burden. Nancy's special attention and her loving words paved way for my easy freedom from the ventilator. Within a few days, I was shifted to mere oxygen. A small oxygen mask was filled with the upper part of the tracheotomy and I had to breathe in.

The angels who attended me during their duty shifts were great support for me. Chinju Chacko, Chinju Sunny, Riya Babu, Merina, Nancy, etc. Sometimes I felt that some others were not interested in accepting me as their 'case'. I felt more courageous while Sheena chechi was in the ICU. After two more days, Nancy would put me in room air. This means leaving me free of the burden of an oxygen mask or ventilator. Gradually, after one day she shifted me to room air completely.

I took it as great pride. Unable to speak out, I discovered a new voice. A voice usually used for beckoning domestic animals like a cat. This was my device for communication till the tracheostomy was removed.

It was Monday, 2 September 2013. I could adapt to the room air for some time.

Morning. VGP said, "Rasith, you can go to the room. Any problem?"

I nodded yes. The doctor asked Nancy to shift to the room and left. I was extremely happy. And Nancy also had the same delight on her face. Sheena chechi too shared her happiness. I realised that the modalities for shifting me to a general room were several. First of them was to pay the bill at the counter. Then there needed to be a vacant room.

My brother struggled hard to gather money for settling the bill. He gathered it somehow. It was in the afternoon a trolley was brought to ICU. The angels picked me up along with the bedsheet and laid me on the trolley. Temporary oxygen connection was also provided. The trolley moved slowly towards the door. The angels bade me goodbye with their confidence-giving smile.

Trolley moved out. The employees in the medical store and security guards also bade farewell. Outside the ICU it was a wider world. The temperature in the general ward was intolerable compared to the ICU. The trolley tripped out from the lift and moved towards the general ward. Before we reached the room, the angels had prepared it, spreading the bedsheet. I was shifted to the bed without much ado. The bed was not so comfortable as it was in the ICU. The airbed here was a little bumpy. I felt a sort of suffocation in the room as if my breath was going out. Blood pressure increased. It was drizzling outside, but in there was quite hot and humid.

The window shutters were open. I couldn't enjoy the sights outside. Through the window, I saw small electric bulbs shining in the distance. Behind the lights, big buildings stand as silhouettes against the sky. I was seeing them for the first time in a month. The rise and fall of blood pressure didn't permit me to enjoy the charm outside.

A laptop and some VCDs had been brought by my brother. I started watching videos at about 1.00 am. Though I had watched the Malayalam movie *Mr. Marumakan* several times, now it seemed to be a new film. I didn't allow my brother to sleep. The job of the angels had to be done by brother. Move my legs, hands, wipe my face, etc., otherwise, the situation was such that my BP would shoot up. I also felt that the nature of care given at ICU was incomparable with that of this ward. As the nursing staff exhibited some disagreements to do suction intermittently, my brother undertook this task too. His quack like activities produced laughter in me.

We didn't have a wink of sleep throughout that night as we watched four movies at night. I tried to control my mind at an optimum level. Since the wee hours, I waited for a sponge bath. None appeared till 8.30 am. They slowly showed themselves up at about 9.00.

After the sponge bath and suction, they returned. The sights outside the room have grown more beautiful then. The blue coloured sky mixed with red colour. Small houses were seen inside the greenery of the distant hill. Human beings were moving as if they were ants when looked from this room. It was at 10 o'clock. A nursing student and her instructor reached there in the same uniform of angels. They asked me about the disease and prepared notes. I didn't like their questions. Therefore, my reply was an expression of repulsion. Still, they had no intention of leaving me alone.

The instructor asked some questions to the student and left the hall. When I understood that I was the subject of her examination, I couldn't control my temper. BP shot up. I gestured my brother to send her out. They didn't pay attention to my demand as they were unaware of my disposition. Another teacher came in. The aforesaid student began to show what they had taught her, treating my body as her tool. It was beyond my tolerance level. My health seemed to break into parts. BP rose; my eyes bulged out; I stared at everyone. Still, they went on with their examination. Finishing it they thanked us and left the room. By this time, the eagles came into the room as a team. 'Eagles' was the name I had given to the therapists.

BP was on the maximum level.

The hospital is going round and round as if in a merry go round.

After constant revolution for a long time, it shrank into a small globe slowly. There was a small ray of light. Junior doctors came running towards me. Father, mother, brother, sister, and brother-in-law who were glad to see my return, were now startled to see me in such a pathetic situation.

A great farewell had been given in the ICU. Therefore, I was quite disturbed to go back to the ICU. Syringes began to once again penetrate my body. Following were ECG, BP checking, and thus there was a saturation fall. The doctor instructed a nurse to bring Ampu bag, which she did in seconds. It was connected to tracheotomy and I was given artificial breath. The doctor instructed them to move me to the ICU immediately.

I was put on a trolley and 'code one' was announced. It is for the smoothness of a patient's shift to ICU, that the doctors usually use the term 'code one'. The trolley moved quickly to ICU.

# 11. Bronchoscopy

I WAS shifted to a ventilator in ICU. The chest showed symptoms of inertia when full mode ventilation was given. It seemed my chest was breaking. On my return, I noticed that there was no air bed. My back was aching. Someone had asked the nurses to switch on the air bed. Dr. Anoop was informed about the air bed. He put me in CPAP and immediately Nancy did everything to ensure the availability of airbed.

VGP came in the evening. He asked, "Kya hua Rasith bhai?"

My reply was a smile that displayed my state of disillusionment. The only moving parts on my body were the thumbs, toes and eyes.

"Rasith, from tomorrow onwards we will start IVIG and by that everything will be alright; don't worry."

I doubted if the old confidence was still in his words. He examined the X-ray film. The angels showed him some problems concerning my chest. Or they expressed their agony when they examined the film. I overheard what VGP whispered to an angel before leaving the hall:

"The chest is completely collapsed; we should do bronchoscopy tomorrow morning itself."

What may be this IVIG? And Bronchoscopy? No idea.

I lay on the bed thinking about these terms at night. Merina came at night for duty. She expanded the term IVIG to me: "Intravenous Immunoglobulin injection. Four phials should be administered four times a day for five days. It is a medicine in liquid form to solve the issues of immunity with antibodies in our body. This liquid is supposed to kill lethal bacteria and viruses in our body. I understood it was costlier than some other injections. One phial costs about Rs. 15,000."

The money in the savings account has been withdrawn. It was the amount I had received from an insurance claim. What shall we do now? I lay on the bed anticipating the worst. Merina went on with her explanation:

"Bronchoscopy is a procedure in which a cleaning tube will be put down the throat to clean the chest of the clotted secretion. When it gets cleaned the saturation will be easier."

Her consoling words gave me more life. She sat near me with her friend Lincy. I felt that it was for the sake of helping me out of the disillusioned situation. Merina had completed her undergraduate programme at Bengaluru. The Christian songs on Lincy's mobile phone were sweet to my ears. I didn't know the passage of time after the sponge bath was over. The morning had dawned. As I had to be taken to the Operation Theatre, I was not given feed that time.

OT uniform was put on me. Nancy prepared me for going to the OT and she waited. I was given feed at neither 11.00 am, and nor at lunchtime. I was taken to the OT two hours after Nancy's duty was over. I was completely tired by then, and I felt as if dizzying darkness overpowered my head. Dr. Praveen supervised bronchostomy. The process began soon. The oxygen mask was removed from the tracheotomy and started suction by a device which had been put down through. It might be because some drug was injected that I didn't feel pain, but I didn't get a breath. The movements of the device could be observed on the monitor when it was thrust down. After the suction was done for sometime oxygen mask was fitted again. Saturation grew up. On the monitor, the saturation level was shown as 100. I was happy. One hour was spent at OT, then I was moved to the ICU. I was confident and at the same time tired too.

Merina was on night duty.

She asked me, "Rasith, should I connect ventilator or oxygen?"

I opted for an oxygen mask. I was given feed immediately. Usually, an injection was given in the evening, but today, they gave me IVIG. Four phials had to be completed. The drug was in a bottle with foaming bubbles. I looked at it entering my body through the cannula. Each drop of the medicine was quite precious. Thus my recovery was getting close. I was quite jubilant that day and observed what was going on in the ICU.

My brother informed me that my company MD had borne the amount needed for IVIG injection. It was a great relief. I didn't know how much I would have to spend more before any recovery. Beyond the thoughts of my illness, I was worried by the thoughts of money. I was coming back to my consciousness too. IVIG injection on the fifth day was also over. The last hope. There is no medicine stronger than this for my ailment.

Both my hands were tied around with various sorts of talisman, by my brother, sister, friends and relatives with prayers for my early recovery from this fatal disease. The angels prayed at churches for my recovery. At last Zamzam, the elixir brought from Mecca was given to me through Ryles tube. It was a sanctified gift from sister Abidatha, whose mother was in the same ICU.

The next day was Onam, the national festival of Kerala. VGP arranged the distribution of payasam. To my surprise, maybe by the grace of God Almighty, I orally tasted some payasam. I felt it going down my throat to the bottom of the stomach with its sweet taste. But after some time I felt a little uneasy. So, through suction, a part of payasam was taken out.

The balance of Zamzam had been kept at home by my brother. Nothing changed still; no change on my legs and hands, no movement at all. The hospital bill was paid at the counter. I ran out of money. I heard a rumour that I was going to be shifted to the hospital at Vadakara, a municipal town, not so distant and costly as that of Kozhikode.

Nancy had resigned her job and Riya joined instead. In no time Riya could take me to room air. I was shifted to the general ward again after two days, this time without much formalities of goodbye.

The shifting to the new ward was late at night. I could adapt to the room temperature, it seems. BP was in control. Chinju Chacko and Chinju Sunny visited me in the morning itself. My delight went up when I saw them. Brother brought my mother to the hospital, and he went for a job especially because there was a crunch of money. And I was feeling better this time. At night, a relative of mine or a friend would stand by me.

In the meantime, my sister and brother-in-law would be present. When I began to see them all I was more relieved as if my illness was getting over. I wanted to prepare mentally to go to the hospital at Vadakara. Some of my relatives are residing near this hospital. Expenses would come down. ICU charges would be lower. From the words of my brother, I could understand that we were out of money. So it was better to adapt to the situation.

I prepared my mind so. Everyone has limitations. I sometimes felt that it was on Radio Mango my heart pulses were living. Even today, I keep the same FM radio set with me. After I left ICU, the angels lost their chance to listen to music on the radio. ICU was calm.

Mother went home for two days. My brother and auntie along with Riju stood by me in the general ward. Riju is the son of my father's younger brother. I had someone to talk with. He has the habit of eating chocolate and groundnut. He would put on my tongue secretly the pieces of dairy milk chocolate.

VGP visited me on the third day.

"Rasith bhai, can we go to Vadakara? Any problem? Nothing to worry, I have discussed with Dr. Mohandas."

I was ready for any option. I nodded positively.

Since that day, my brother began new experiments. Instead of doing suction, he asked me to spit out the saliva. I was not able to do so, but when saliva comes out it could be wiped with some towel or so. At times he would display how to take in saliva. But the smell of my saliva was quite bad. How could I explain it to them?

While I was in ICU my BP would go up to 230. Then my brother would use some tricks to bring it down. He would ask me to count down from 100 to 0. If urination is difficult, imagine a water tap is turned on and water is flowing out. Those tricks became some kinds of jokes to reduce my BP. Who has time for thinking when the mind is completely occupied with tormenting visions?

The world is going round and round! There was no problem that night. Next day VGP came there and instructed the nurses to prepare the discharge sheet.

At noon, when all the bills had been paid, an ambulance reached the front gate near the reception area to take me to the hospital at Vadakara. Chinju Chacko and Riya visited me to bid farewell from there. They asked me to remain calm. The trolley was taken to the porch through the elevator.

I closed my eyes tightly, unable to look at the light outside. Still, it appeared that sunlight was intruding my eyes. It was the first time after three months that I came out of the cooled room of this hospital. An ambulance stopped in front of me. I opened my eyes slowly. My body was hot all over like the red hot iron. I was slowly shifted to the ambulance.

My auntie got into the vehicle and sat beside me while my brother occupied the front seat near the driver. It was an ordinary ambulance. It entered the road with a loud siren. We were followed by my brother-in-law in his Maruti car. I had great fear inside. An ambulance with no modern facilities. In the case of BP going up, an incident of suffocation or breathlessness, no way to resolve. I controlled my mind, with the thought "come what may".

I asked my brother to switch on the radio and tune on Radio Mango. The ambulance ran through the streets of Kozhikode city with siren and radio songs. I lay there enjoying the songs from the radio channel.

In one hour, the ambulance reached co-operative hospital premises at Vadakara. No change in BP level. But it was scorching heat there. I was taken out of the vehicle and put on the trolley. The trolley had been brought there by some middle-aged attendants. With a tube into the nose and tracheostomy on the throat I was emaciated and lean. Seeing such a pathetic plight was quite embarrassing to the outsiders from the rural areas. Still, I had the same smile on my face. The trolley moved to Dr. Mohandas' consultation room.

We didn't have to wait at all as VGP had informed him of my arrival. He began his examination using the same hammer-like instrument tapping on my knees and arms. I was headed to the ICU that was on the ground floor. When someone opened the glass door, I heard a piece of wonderfully sweet music. With the help of angels, I was shifted to the bed. Compared to the ICU at BMH, this room was like a general ward of BMH.

To raise the head part of the bed, the handle had to be rotated. I doubted if the air conditioner was working. The rent for the room was lower than that of BMH. Despite all, all the angels in the hospital reached there to see the patient on whom tracheostomy was done. I couldn't see what was happening in the ICU. At BMH whenever I wanted, visitors were allowed.

At ICU, they put me on oxygen for some time. Though I looked for ventilator it was not seen anywhere. Therefore, my moves were quite careful. I got food through Ryles tube from there. Every item was available like wheat porridge, rice porridge, Horlicks, juice, etc. However, the angels there were not ready to give them orally.

They would just take it for granted that these food items were unwanted. When we ask for the dishes, they would empty the food from them and return the dishes. They helped me remove the saliva spread over the lips and chin only rarely. Even this would be done on my insistence, sometimes.

Yet, I didn't feel angry with anyone because I knew that there was no ventilator in case my saturation level fell below the normal level. I felt ICU a place for those who were about to die. Majority of the inpatients there were suffering from fatal diseases. They go back with their still bodies. I witnessed various signals of death and was completely startled. My thoughts were just to get out of this ICU somehow.

I could count every moment of all the 18 days spent in this room. I was shifted to the private ward. Air bed and cot were ready there. The door had a sticker that said, 'visitors not allowed'. The flow of visitors went down. Only mouth care was available in the room. The remaining care had been done by my mother, sister and brother. I was able to lean against the pillow if the head part of the bed was raised.

I took it as a pride. I could sit only 10 minutes at a time. Its duration was enhanced slowly. Therapy was done at an interval of one hour. My sister was the therapist. Electric supply was available at Vadakara town for 4-5 hours a day on those days. It was quite a relief that I got back my FM radio when I came back to the room. I listened to the radio every time. For doing suction, there was only one machine. After I got admitted there, they had to keep it in my room.

The next day when the doctor came for the round he asked the nurses to remove the urine bag. It was the happiest moment in my hospital life. The attempt to remove at least one tube had been successful! There remain two more tubes, Ryles and tracheostomy tubes. Dr. Mohandas said that they would also be removed soon.

Another obstacle I faced there was the inability to take in saliva as normal human beings do. I was wondering wherefrom this much of secretion came. It had been four months since I was admitted to the hospital. Without interval, saliva had been secreted continuously like the immortal flow from a fountain. Now I was able to sit against something for 15 minutes continuously. Nebulisation must be done two times a day. I felt nebulisation as a great hurdle especially the device and medicine had to be brought from Kozhikode every time.

I experienced strong suffocation while nebu was inhaled. Sometimes it was possible to do nebulisation by removing the oxygen mask at times. I could spend 25 days in room air without much danger. After ten days of my inpatient life in this room, some breathing problem had started. While physiotherapy was being done, blood pressure shot up. The doctor prescribed an X-ray. On getting the laboratory report, I heard the doctor telling my brother:

"His chest has collapsed again. Bronchoscopy must be done. But, we don't have enough facility here. You'd rather go to BMH."

Disillusionment gripped me once again. I was informed about this, and they suggested that we could return by the evening to BMH.

# 12. Again to BMH

ON 4 November, I prepared for the next trip to BMH. Though the doctor had told us that something troubled my chest, I was not ready to put on an oxygen mask. I tried to strengthen my mind. The trolley was brought at 11.00 am and an ambulance was ready at the porch. The same ordinary ambulance, but I was not excited or fearful when I got into the ambulance. My mental energy seemed to be stronger this time. Nothing troubled my mind. Come what may!

I was aware that there was not much improvement in my condition even after four months of treatment. My hopes were almost shattered. Nevertheless, my confidence has not faded from my face. The ambulance was running fast and I lay in enjoying the green fields on the sides of the national highway.

I saw plastic boards known as flex boards, trees, fashion advertisements, passing vehicles, etc., on both sides of the national highway. The songs from the FM station were so melodious.

The ambulance reached BMH, at 1.45 pm. I felt a little annoyance in going back to the ICU there. The men in blue uniform approached with the trolley. The urine bag removal was a great change for me. I was taken to the Neuro ICU. I could see smiling faces of the patients as well as others in the room as if they were enjoying a joke.

Yet, they did their service well. When they tried to put on oxygen mask I prevented them. It seemed they were not willing to speak to me. During the time of suction, they would simply smile and do it in silence contrary to the previous stay here. I was happy when Chinju Chacko arrived.

I got someone to chat with. She was not in charge of my care, but I called her often and make her do suction. I wanted to go back to the ordinary ward.

My brother told me that we could return to Vadakara today itself. This gave me great relief. I was not provided with food in preparation to go to OT. I was tired. By the time I reached the OT, it was 5.00 pm and Dr. Praveen was there to perform a bronchoscopy. It took not much time to do it and I knew that chest was completely infected with saliva. When it was completely removed, the saturation level displayed 100 per cent on the monitor. As it was quite late when I was transferred to the ICU, we couldn't go back to Vadakara. But I was angry. So I had to vent my anger on others, this time on Chinju Sunny. My body seemed to be shaky due to fever.

I was put on a bed at the extreme corner of the ICU. It was possible to see the outside view more clearly. Heavy rain had started. Thunder and lightning characteristic of the monsoon month of Thulam escorted it. I was unable to enjoy rain; the mind has started being restless. I should go to Vadakara somehow. VGP came to examine me. He used his small torch and thermometer to see if I had a fever. Sample of secretion was sent to the laboratory for examination.

"Rasith bhai, you can go to Vadakara after two days," said VGP.

At night Riya took care of me. I asked her why VGP said so.

"It's because the secretion sample has been sent to the lab for examination. After getting the report, you'll be shifted to a room today itself. Don't worry."

However, I was not convinced by her reply. I lay there looking at the raindrops showering outside. I was shivering all over and my body was extremely hot. In the evening came Chinju Chacko. There was another angel too. She looked like an experienced woman. Her behaviour was quite lively. But her words were not so mild. I asked Chinju about her.

"That is Jisha chechi, and she is as senior as Sheena chechi. She was on leave for some days. She joined when Rasith had gone to Vadakara."

Jisha chechi had been watching us. She asked:

"Why does he need suction? You come here and attend other patients now."

Her joke was a little cruel, or so it seemed to me. I want to go to the room. I lay there some time without talking to anyone. VGP came again. Chinju showed him the lab report. When they were discussing the report, I was not able to hear well.

"Rasith bhai, you can go to your room after some time."

After VGP left the room, they injected some drugs on my body. This time they did it through the cannula. I experienced a boiling sensation in the body. I got relief when the injection was over. When I asked about the lab report, Sheena chechi and Chinju replied, "No problem."

Yet, I overheard them conversing a little away from my bedside. They were talking about an injection named 'Amikacin'. But I didn't ask them about what I heard. They shifted me at 8.00 pm.

It was quite a relief to come to a room. The nursing supervisor Lissy visited me and spent some time there. Dalia was on duty that night. She did the suction and gave me food. My exhaustion and fever were not over yet. I asked Dalia about the injection. She explained that Amikacin was normally given to patients of pneumonia. When I heard this, I was more shocked because Vivi had cautioned me about pneumonia. How could I escape? Why did new health issues prop up one after another?

There was heavy rain outside, and thunder and lightning accompanying. Perhaps nature was celebrating itself, but inside me, the temperature is going up. I was shivering. Dalia contacted VGP and gave me an injection. However, the fever didn't subside. They put ice cubes on my body till about 3 am to cool off the temperature.

The next three days it continued. Breath came back to the normal. On the fifth day, VGP permitted to go back to Vadakara. Still, I didn't have the same confidence to go back to Vadakara. I knew there were no facilities there to address the issues that might come up again after some time. What should I do if pneumonia came back? Still, I didn't say no to the permission because we had already run out of money this time too.

Again on an ambulance. I lay indifferently, seeing through the glass the sights outside. We went directly to the ward at the hospital. The angel from the ICU was on duty there. She was a little short with clipped teeth. I didn't know her name yet. She had a modest way of talking along with loving behaviour. When I leaned against on the bed, I felt more comfortable on my chest. Physiotherapy was done every hour. Fever subsided; antibiotics stopped.

"Before removing tracheotomy, water should be served orally," Dr. Mohandas gave instructions to the nurse.

An angel immediately brought some water and poured into my mouth, but I was unable to take it down. When some cough deflated, a little water went down. Then again, it was repeated. It was the first time after four months, water went down my throat physically. I could see the happiness on the faces of all. My brother was asking the doctor if it was possible to give some juice or anything similar. The doctor prevented it by saying:

"Only water, at intervals. Then you can give him oral rehydration solutions (ORS) so that he could taste and saltwater would heal the small sores in the throat."

Therapy started again. Now I could sit leaning against the head part of the bed. Visitors were allowed; the outside sights were growing green, gradually.

A positive change for the good. Urine bag was removed. I can recline on the bed, drink a little water. As a first step to remove tracheostomy, they started covering the hole with some bandage.

"We should avoid tracheostomy completely in 10 days."

When I heard the doctor's words, I was extremely delighted mainly for the reason that then I could talk. After coming to the hospital, my mother and brother wouldn't do what I had asked them. When I felt angry, I would lay calm. It was now going to end. The feeding duty was taken over by my brother. Therefore, whenever I was hungry, the feed was given. Happy days, nights. I reached in such a state wherein I could sleep for a while.

On the fourth day, I could sit on the bed after therapy. I felt a strong cough after some time. Reason unknown. As if some obstacle was on the throat. I thought it was a Ryles tube. The doctor said it might be that of tracheostomy. I was able to sit that day for some time. When some days passed, I wasn't able to even get up and therapy was also impossible. It was prevented by a dry cough. I noticed that I was going back to the previous state. Fluctuation in BP, suffocation, loss of sleep, etc.

"Tomorrow we'll remove the Ryles tube. Then your cough will stop and let us continue physiotherapy." Doctor's words were quite motivating. The next day, body temperature went up.

Shivering too. A sign of danger again. It was again the symptoms of pneumonia. Amikacin was given, and the body was cool. Brother had left for home. He would come back the next day. BP was on the increase. I was not able to enjoy music on the radio. Spent time on bed observing my breath in and out sleeplessly.

In the morning brother came back. Tracheostomy was closed and an angel measured saturation level and she saw that it had gone down to 70 per cent. Tracheostomy plastic was removed and checked the saturation level and saw the level was still down. The angel briefed my brother about the new developments and she brought an oxygen cylinder. She provided me with an oxygen mask. Still, I felt breathless. My physique was scorching. The desperate state of mine spread a pall of gloom on those who were watching me. When I fumbled for breath, I began to throw my head sideways. It was then the new angel with dental braces came towards us. She inspected the cylinder and said that it was empty.

"Please bring a new cylinder before the saturation level falls further," she entreated.

The angels went out in haste. I could not control anger as well as sorrow. BP had shot up. The hospital was completely revolving. It reached a point after several rounds of revolution. There was a small light that spread across all corners of the hospital. I heard a crowd calling out at me and their loud noises. Something was moving as if a faded shadow. Suddenly, the light dimmed. Darkness was everywhere, and everything came to complete silence.

# 13. Face to face with death

I CAME back to consciousness again. Then I found myself in ICU. I saw people in dim light walking here and there. Two doctors were giving directions. Breath has halted completely. I was getting artificial breath through Ambu bag and oxygen. Saturation level has come down as low as 55.

When Ambu bag was removed, I did not get a breath. I felt it quite difficult to breathe with the help of an oxygen mask. They didn't heed my request to remove it. BP was on the increase again. When I was facing death, my mother's and brother's faces were seen as if behind a screen.

I saw gesticulations of a hysteric patient on her face. Brother's face was pale, probably, out of fear. I tried to smile to make them consoled. When Ambu continued some more time, the saturation level reached above 80. With this, blood pressure began to get down. The doctor realized that I knew about it and he turned the monitor towards me. However, saturation did not go up beyond 85. I again saw my brother contacting BMH.

Together with Ambu bag, the stretcher got out of the ICU. It seemed that those who were waiting outside were shocked at my state of health. I didn't pay attention to them. If so, my BP would have gone up again. As soon as the stretcher reached the porch, an ambulance was there. It was a mobile ICU.

There were all the facilities, apart from the oxygen cylinder. Two doctors and an assistant got in with us in the ambulance. If BP goes up, the condition was unpredictable. They connected the oxygen mask to the tracheostomy. After taking in breath for some time, I felt tired. I tried to control my mind by looking outside, to control BP as far as possible. I assured myself for a strong comeback.

It took 45 minutes to bring back BP to the normal level. In one hour, the ambulance reached BMH at Kozhikode. The attendants in a blue uniform rushed towards the ambulance with a stretcher. They rushed me to the emergency ward, instead of ICU. The junior doctors started their examination. An X-ray was prescribed after half an hour and still, we had to wait for long. I got angry and so shouted to one of the junior doctors for not taking me to the ICU.

It was thus a trolley was ordered, and a trolley with a ventilator rushed to the ICU where I saw the security women and other members of hospital staff looking at me indifferently.

I could see an amusing smile spreading on the face of a duty nurse on my new return. Yet I did not seriously pay attention to it. The angels left the room shifting me to the bed. A towel was placed on the upper side of the bed for spitting the saliva. They kept it over there by saying that it was a kind of exercise. But it caused great discomfort to me because several times I happened to lie on the towel-covered with saliva.

Dr. Anoop came rushing towards me in five minutes.

"Why did you keep a towel beside your head? In the case of secretion from the mouth, it should be wiped out immediately. Ventilation arrangements should not be changed without my consent."

He asked an angel to bring a cannula. It was a little bigger. He brought it to my neck side and injected it into the artery. It was not so painful and he joined it with a 'three-way'. It was at this same point they had put the central line on my first visit to BMH. A central line was usually placed when a patient was medicated with antibiotic continually. A blood sample could also be taken out when needed. I began to receive the status of a VIP patient at ICU. Several medicines were injected into my body. The angels gave protein powder every hour, besides the usual feed. Dr. Anoop could bring back my self-confidence in one hour though I was completely hopeless about my health. He also examined me at short intervals.

My soul whispered to me, "I will come back."

On his instruction, I had been getting chest therapy incomparable to the previous ones. For 15 minutes, a young man did therapy by hitting me hard on the chest.

"Tomorrow Rasith will undergo Bronchoscopy. With this, everything will be okay."

Merina was put on duty. I told her everything about the hospital at Vadakara. I had nothing to fear at night due to the reason that whoever was put on duty would remain with me and they would serve me with protein powder every hour.

Bronchoscopy was done the next day. When I returned, he began to remove tracheotomy tube slowly; though I was a little frightened at first, his presence helped me to overcome this fear. Sheena chechi inserted a Ryles tube removing the old one. A new machine was connected to tracheotomy instead of the ventilator. Despite having difficulty at first, I understood later that to breathe in was easier than while on a ventilator. When Dr. Anoop left the ICU, I asked about this machine to Merina.

"This is BPAP. You are free from ventilator now. Do you have breathing difficulty with this machine? You'll be shifted to the room tomorrow."

I recalled VGP and Vivi's words: "If removed from the ventilator, half of the way is done."

I opened my FB on my brother's mobile phone and posted:

"I'm coming back."

I hadn't forgotten the Malayalam short film *Thorthu* shown by brother Ansal. I experienced the unbearable chill at ICU. First time after four months, I put on a T-shirt. I asked Chinju to cover me with a blanket.

"Brother, I have a duty in the morning, and you'll have food orally."

It was with happiness, I bade goodbye to her.

VGP came in the morning.

Rasith bhai, let's not go back to Vadakara, instead, you'll go home after you get well. You'll be shifted to the room today. My happiness knew no bounds listening to his words. I began to feel nostalgic. What would have happened to my home and my locality? I began to imbibe the thoughts of returning home.

Dr. Anoop removed the BPAP for some time and kept me in the room air. I asked for some juice to Chinju Chacko. In ten minutes my brother brought some juice. Sheena chechi took the juice in a spoon and brought to my mouth. I finished a cup of juice. I could feel the drops of juice going down my throat reaching my stomach. Oral food was mixed with pulses for lunch. I liked it. I felt an appetite for it and asked Chinju to give me some. She ordered a cup of pulses from the canteen.

I ate it completely within an hour. I drank a little water too. I began to observe ICU as if I was victorious. I began to get chocolate pieces and banana fry as oral intake of food started. In the evening, a trolley was brought and I was shifted to the room in room air itself. A new angel reached there to receive me in the room. Her name was on the badge she wore on her coat: 'Sadiya Saleem'.

She left the room after doing suction and connecting BPAP even without my request for them. As if in a dark shadow, my body began to boil that night. Again pneumonia. The doctor prescribed paracetamol injection. No change yet in body temperature. Breathless still. I began to throw my head sideways. Brother was called in. When he arrived, I was sweltering with loss of breath. He seemed to be angry.

"What do you want? Do you want to enjoy the comforts of ICU always?" he asked.

They did not know the 'comfort' of a ventilator. Air usually lashed into my chest! Everyone would tend to survive. The angels examined the saturation level and I understood that it was not the lack of respiration, but excessive heartbeat rate that had gone up to150.

I was asked to take in a breath slowly. It might be because of pneumonia. They put ice cubes in a small plastic bag and began to cool my body. At 2.00 am, fever subsided and slept for a short while.

At five o'clock I woke up. Heartbeat came back to normal. I looked outside leaning against the pillow. The rain had heavily showered in at night. The world has become more beautiful. Drops of rain have been falling from the parapet. Sunlight had thrown varied colours in the sky. Birds were flying to an unknown destination in batches. Sun had started coming up.

After several months, I could enjoy everything. Songs from FM radio had sweetened the background. With increased confidence, I demanded uzhunnu vada. However, I could eat only a small piece. I was able to eat. My next job was to think about what item I should order. After physiotherapy by my brother that night, I tried to move my hands strongly.

As if with divine power, my left palm fell on one side. I couldn't believe it at first I tried again. True, it was moving. A madness of delight had started to overpower me. Without telling anyone, I moved it again in the dim light. Right palm, too, had started moving. Outside,

Thula Varsham was falling heavily. There was a heavy thunder with lightning as if nature was dancing with delight.

Next morning, I showed my mother and brother how the hands were moving. Dr. Anoop examined my hands and legs. He said: "We are going to close tracheotomy for some time. You must breathe in air through your nose. If tracheotomy is closed, you could also speak well."

He dressed tracheotomy with a cork and asked my name. He asked me to repeat loudly. "Rasith," I said in the loudest voice. Though the tongue didn't co-operate well, I could speak out and one more obstacle was over.

Dr. Anoop had gone back. I got the telephone number of Neuro ICU; knowing not how to share this happiness, I dialled the number; Merina answered my phone.

"Good morning, Neuro ICU. May I help you?"

"Good morning madam, I'm Fr. Ignatius. I would like to know the details about one patient," I said authoritatively with an experienced tone.

The silence was the reply on the other end. Then I asked if she knew who she was talking to. I revealed my identity.

"I'm Rasith."

Again the same silence.

I heard Merina expressing her gratitude to Jesus Christ. My mind got better concentration after talking to several people thus. I consumed several kinds of dishes that day. One of the angels asked my mother if they could remove the Ryles tube. She nodded ‘yes’.

My brother had gone out. Mother contacted him over a mobile phone. He was not ready to concede their demand. He thought that it would be dangerous if I couldn’t drink water. My mother knew me well. If my confidence said one thing, I wouldn’t argue with others to fulfil it. Instead, I would do it practically.

Especially then, my body was in control of my mind step by step. I called the angel and asked her to remove the Ryles tube. Sadiya immediately did so. Another burden from my body had been removed. Disappointment gained more ease. I began to eat food prepared at home by my sister. I drank more water.

In the evening Merina and Riya along with Chinju visited me. We chatted for some time. In the following two days, BPAP was avoided.

# 14. To Mundakkutty

DR. ANOOP and Daliya came to my room on 28 November. She examined BP and saturation level and confirmed as normal. Dr. Anoop untied the knot of the tracheostomy tube from my neck. He slowly removed the tube and cleaned the area with sterile water. The small hole was covered with cotton and plastered well. I didn't have much pain. Thus the last tube from my body had been removed. He cleaned this hole continuously for three days and dressed well.

The third-day VGP said,

"Rasith bhai, don't you want to go home? Tomorrow you can go."

I was completely astonished. My delight was inexplicable.

On Monday, 2 December 2013, VGP examined me and went back to ICU. He instructed me to visit BMH for review after one month.

There was another patient, Usha, with GBS in ICU.

After some time Dr. Anoop changed my dressing on the throat and fixed a new one asking me not to wet it for two weeks.

"While taking bath it should be covered properly. If you need anything, don't forget to call me."

I always felt a difference in his words and behaviour.

By noon mother began to prepare for our discharge and departure from the hospital. My cousin Niraj and my brother-in-law came over there. Together with my brother, they were in a hurry to arrange the hospital bill to pay at the counter. Sadiya came there to bid me farewell while she was leaving the hospital after her morning duty. I called Sheena chechi to ICU in the afternoon. I told her in Kannada that I was leaving the hospital.

"Hey Rasith, go home and from there you will be able to walk soon. All the best."

She was unable to speak in a low voice. After the bill was settled and received the discharge summary. It was six o'clock before the trolley arrived. My brother and brother-in-law took me up and seated me in the front, near the driver seat, helping to wear the seatbelt. Brother and mother got into our car.

Brother-in-law and my sister travelled in their car. The car slowly rolled on to the street and I looked back and read the name Baby Memorial Hospital in the limelight of the city flooded in neon light. I looked at it again. They again have immersed in their busy world. The car was speeding along the crowded streets of Kozhikode.

In July last year, this car had the same momentum. I had called it a day when I was so paralysed. There was heavy rain along the street. Enjoying the coloured light from the grand shopping malls, I leaned back in my seat.

The car was moving quite slowly now. My happiness was similar to the one who was released after several months of imprisonment. I was tired of sitting for a long time. When we reached Perambra, the car stopped and moved my hands and legs before sitting afresh. This was the town I had roamed along with my friends and called out slogans while studying at CKGM College during my undergraduate study.

In the first year, I had been elected as a student representative. In the second year of study, I contested the election but tasted defeat. In the final year too, I was elected as general secretary.

I have recollected the memories of love, struggle, writing, and learning during my student life at this college. Five minutes of reverie about beautiful college life. Around 8.30 pm we passed Kuttiady, heading for my native village, Mundakkutty.

All the sights outside had gained an inexplicable beauty. In half an hour we got into the pathway to my house from where two persons standing outside the car and another from the car carried me in their hands to take me to the bed prepared for me at my house.

The air bed that I had purchased from Vadakara had been set up with a new bedsheet. The fan and television had been arranged at the places convenient for me. I would be given food on the bed making me lean against someone. I was in a state of security as there would be someone with me always during the night to help me lie sideways (on either side). I would fall from my bed sometimes.

From day one, I saw a flood of visitors whose talk, comments, facial expressions, etc., could be interestingly observed by me. They gave me advice, instructions, explanations, along with tears welling in their eyes often.

At every one-hour interval, my sister would do physiotherapy so that I could move my limbs a little more vigorously. However, hands could not be lifted from the bed. From morning until sleeping at night, I would lie on the bed watching programmes on TV.

The appetite for food increased gradually. Sometimes my friends would bring parcelled food from restaurants. It seemed the days were waning fast. On 31 December, I enjoyed the programmes celebrating the New Year until about 1.00 am. Mundakkutty village was also completely enjoying like me.

Several months have gone by after I had a good bath and cleaned my teeth. My mother helped me clean my teeth, fed me every time as if I was a young child. When I had my first bath here, I understood that it was quite a terrible job. In the bathroom I was seated on a wooden chair; water would be showered on me; then I felt a little frightened. The part where tracheostomy was done was covered.

I sometimes felt suffocation. Some water would be poured and before another mug was poured, I would have to wait for some time. Then I would open my eyes and breathe in the air, like a child. However, after a good bath, I was quite energetic. For the first time, I had a good nap at noon. The time had started quickly passing.

I began to pass time by observing how the sprouting of leaves was taking place in the palm tree planted outside of my house. I had studied the novel *The Woodlanders* by Thomas Hardy while I was an undergraduate student. I remembered the novel while observing the leaves on the palm tree. The protagonist was a man of superstition; the wood that he saw outside would come down one day. He believed that at that moment his life would end. If it happened exactly as per his conviction or not, Thomas Hardy does not say in the novel.

It seemed to have awakened my long-forgotten poetic creativity. My hands were incapable of writing. I was not willing to get the help of a scribe in writing what I dictate. My mind had been raked with the thought of penning down my experience. What had troubled me more was my inability to put down the thoughts into words than my bedridden body and paralysed limbs.

# 15. Physiotherapy

EVERYONE ASSOCIATED with me was in search of a physiotherapist. At last, on January 2, Monday evening came the therapist. He seemed to be mature and remained so throughout the therapy. He was a physiotherapist from the Pain and Palliative Care Unit of Kuttiady.

He belonged to Vanimel, Nadapuram in our district. Since two people heading towards one aim travelling along two pathways, a new intimate friendship grew up between us. Though others might think about me as a patient, I was not interested in considering me as a patient myself. Luckily, I got a therapist who had a similar point of view.

More than being a therapist, he was my true friend. Along with this intimacy, the treatment progressed. I never can forget the wheelchair donated by the Palliative Care Unit. I could slowly come out of the bedroom and sit in front of the veranda.

The waning rays of sunset piercing through the foliage, fog, Vannathi Pullu birds that visited our house in search of small preys in the morning and evening, etc, began to flower into poetic lines. One of these birds used to peck from grains at the kitchen. Mother used to interpret this by saying that it was the spirit of my grandmother. Therefore, it enjoyed a special consideration concerning its food.

I was not able to spend more than one hour on the wheelchair. I got two assistants to take me back to bed. Anand and Adarsh were my neighbours. It was Adarsh who started to write down my poems on paper. When he sang those lines, during a school farewell party, he got very good appreciation. It was a great encouragement for me.

Hussain had the cumbersome task of rejuvenating my veins and neural network. No one was satisfied with his initial therapy because he began it with an attempt to move my hands and legs for at least half an hour.

What transformation could it make on my body? They doubted. I too doubted it.

A hard and continuous effort for one month could make me spread my hands along the bed. Slowly, he adopted a new technique to bring the upper part of my body under my control by enabling me to sit on the bed. If I lean against one side more time, I would fall flat losing my balance.

Within a few days, minor changes began to show up. My speech grew more legible. I understood that the tracheostomy area was being healed. Therefore, the band-aid put there was removed. This part later became a small hole and finally turned into a small unnoticeable mark. In about two months, I could raise both my hands well. When I reached a state in which I was able to control my body while sitting, I slowly began to stand against the wall myself.

Still, there was no change in the paralysed state of my legs. If my knee happens to bend while making me stand against the wall, no one could make it straight. Likewise, one day I fell on my left side hitting on the tip of my bed. Despite great pain, I did not dare to tell anyone about it. Instead, I reminded my mind that I aimed to get up and walk normally.

April was quite a heavy month for me due to its scorching weather condition. I was sweating every time due to my endless hard work to regain the virility. I was disappointed by the fact that the legs did not move, as I desired. By the end of May, I could move the hands powerfully along with the fingers. I discovered my old Samsung Wave 3 smartphone and got connected through the internet, and I started contacting my friends through FB to share my tragic experience with them.

Nature, the birds, the flowers, and everything around me bloomed into beautiful flowers on the pages of FB. I began to write the loose jokes that we had enjoyed during my college education at CKGM College, Perambra. My fingers were unable to coordinate with my mental status, to translate them on to the paper.

I wrote them in Manglish. Yet, those who read the post gave their comments and feedback ingraining them with appreciation and encouragement. This gave me an impetus to bring back the world of writing which had been long forgotten during my job in Bengaluru.

Still, I was haunted by an indefinable hollowness inside. My legs and hip did not show any sign of mobility. The future course of my life also seems quite indefinite.

The Malayalam month of Meenam gave way to the noisy, dynamic and rainy Edavapathy (the month of torrential rain). I am now able to sit on the chair for more time. I can control my body better than before. The small bird visitors stepped into the water, flipped and splashed, shared love among themselves which was a wonderful scene in front of me. After each shower of heavy rain, a dark shadow spread far and wide in my world.

There were landslides in the heavy climate of monsoon in my locality, especially at the hilly areas of Pasukkadavu. There were news reports of climatic havocs everywhere. Hussain's burden increased. Giving me more hopes, the left leg showed signs of movement. At the end of hard efforts, I could stand on both the legs which enhanced my confidence. This recovery is beyond my expectation and this gave me more hopes.

Someone whispered into my ears, "Yeah, you will come back, you will come back."

Because the nerves had completely died, it was an adventurous task to make my body stand straight. However, Hussain did his duty with commitment and greater responsibility. The review visits to the hospital were limited to once in two months. Medicines were reduced. The treatment for months on end had financially and mentally devastated me. How long should I continue the treatment? To get the ability to move with legs, therapy is required for several days.

Edavappathy subsided. And after Mithunam, the darkest rainy season called Karkidakam took over.

There remains a "What next?" question in front of me. But I hadn't lost hope on the confidence that I can find success in every job that I undertake. Loneliness has gripped me over. The fifth day after 'Vavu Bali', heavy rain battered the earth's bosom. While I was having breakfast after a bath, a two-wheeler reached my porch.

The man who got out from the scooter removed his water-drenched raincoat and helmet, stepped on to the veranda and said: "We don't know each other. We are meeting for the first time."

Though it was our first meeting, I felt an age-old intimacy in his presence. He was clad in a tall kurtha and dhoti. A chain of rudraksha around the neck and vermillion on his forehead. He looked like a swami. He began to introduce himself to me:

"I'm Shaneesh R Nair. I studied at CKGM College in the senior batch."

I recalled the friend request on FB some months ago. He moved a chair near my wheelchair and started talking.

It was an energising talk that Shaneesh has made. In his words, I could discover some positive points that would make my future brighter. The emptiness is gradually fading, and I have started chirping on the lovely memories of student life at CKGM College. A new wave of intimate friendship has started to encompass my life. I got a smartphone as a token of love from my friends.

Then, the lines I had penned down began to get wings and fly on to the world of fantasy. The exuberant mind's overflow into poetic lines and short stories. I took it a mission to write about Guillain-Barre Syndrome, which had overturned my life. The texts typed on the smartphone were sent as SMS to my friends. The poetic lines flowered into gazals at the hands of advocate Vineesh and Prabheesh. Later, my thoughts were how to transform a smartphone into a useful device with its unseen potential. This was because I had no other way out.

When one door was closed, a hundred doors would open in front of us. This was my thought.

The Malayalam year opened with the month of Chingam. Atham started new spring with the flowery memories of Onam, the national festival of Kerala. During the Onam festival, my CKGM College friends visited me. For the first time in my life, I got six pairs of clothes! Plantain leaves were spread in front of my guests for catering food.

I also tried to have the sadya with my friends. Taking the morsels of rice in my hand, I began to fetch it to my mouth with great difficulty. Though I couldn't take it in a lump, I finished eating in one hour. They all waited for me until I finished it. Thus after one year of the interval, I was able to eat satisfactorily on my own.

# 16. She was waiting for me

BEGINNING TO write the memorable experiences at the ICU of Baby Memorial Hospital, my restlessness seemed to be toning down. Such complicated and deadly situations were translated into words without losing their intensity. The day and nights were transformed into solitude, and I searched the most appropriate expressions.

It almost seemed that I had conquered Guillain-Barre Syndrome.

Along with this, I intensified the physical exercises. By October 15, I was able to take some steps forward with my legs. My mother celebrated this day by arranging a party to the physiotherapist. There was a lot to do before I come back to normalcy. I was unable to walk without support. The fact that I could at least walk gave me great hope and confidence that I could regain my health even if it was slow.

This was not sudden anyway. I had fallen on the floor at least eight times in a month before being able to walk myself on the feet. Yet, I did not relinquish. Sometimes when I fell, I could notice the wounds and blood on my knees. By November, I was able to walk slowly in my house without much assistance though my footsteps were like toddlers. As I got more strength on my knees, the frequency of falling decreased.

Thula Varsham was over. Thus, the heavy rainy season had its last step out in Kerala until the next year. As the weather was slowly getting into normalcy, Hussain took me to the courtyard and helped me walk around my house. The backyard of my house seemed to be unfamiliar to me. The small mounts and gutters in my courtyard were quite difficult for me to tread on. He made me walk at least two times a day. In one week, I was in control of my steps too. Gradually I could step on to the pathway to my house. We would walk 50 metres and sit on the small bridge over a creek.

Other than physical exercises, I could increasingly connect to the people of my village too. Mental energy shot up. My next efforts were to visit BMH next time on my own.

I had chatted with Jaffar and Molly about agriculture as a fun, which later became a serious affair. I began to plant various types of plantain and tapioca. I watched them growing up minutely. This was a unique sort of satisfaction. I firmly planned to go forward with my agenda of fostering agriculture in future when I recover completely. My dream took various shapes as I wandered through the vast space of friendship, agriculture, literature, etc, leaving aside the narrow dreams I had when I was in Bengaluru.

In the foggy December, I got a new friend. His name was N.S. Sajith, a staff of Deshabhimani newspaper.

For an article about 'Panappayatt' on Facebook, I got great appreciation. I had been asked to write an article in the Deshabhimani special supplement about war, violence and cinema during IFFK 2014. An article was written with the title 'The Infinite Possibilities of Action' about *Windtalkers*, a war movie, and it was published in Deshabhimani special supplement.

I was being recognised as a writer, therefore, Sajith asked me to write about Guillain-Barre Syndrome and publish a book.

My friends copied the 'Manglish' version of my SMS texts into pure Malayalam. Since then, I began to spend time for physical exercise and writing. Together with Hussain, I had a stroll towards Janaki Forest, the nearest local forest area, and Peruvannamuzhi, a nearby dam site. Water was scarce in the dam. Even the scorching couldn't tire me. From the top bridge of the dam, I copied the beautiful hilly landscape in my camera. From Kuttiady we ate chicken fry and chapati. I walked with the support of my friends along with the Kuttiady town.

Leaving half of 2013 and full 2014 behind, a new year again gave hopes of happiness and varied sights. Everywhere there were celebrations and even the birds joined with them.

Before the celebrations and happiness had died down, music director Advocate Vineesh, singer Prabheesh and dancer Simmi Sandeep joined to render my poetic lines into gazals with the music of Vineesh. It was one of my memorable experiences. In one day, we produced six songs.

Hussain arrived there a little late.

There was spectacular splendour of the rural life spread in the twilight and we walked forward, enjoying them to the full. The women going home from their day labour recognised my attempts to walk along the road, with their smiles. Together with Hussain, I continued my stroll. The muscles got a little more strengthened. I could walk at least 100 strides without assistance. Gradually, I started visiting my neighbourhood. I would take two hours to come back, though. It was exhilarating to visit the nearby houses and accept their reception.

The month of January was severely cool at that time. Even the sun rays seemed to be hesitating to triumph over the chill. My physique was almost frozen after the morning shower. But my mind was warmer. We were about to go for a journey. Sujeesh and his wife Priya came here to take me with them.

Putting on a new pair of clothes after breakfast, we left the house for attending Sindhu's house warming party, from there to Muthukad with my college mates. Muthukad seemed to have changed a lot. Earlier its ambience was completely like that of a forest.

There were concrete buildings on both sides of the road. Our car moved forward along the spiralling hilly road. In the dense forest, he was hiding somewhere. Satheesh Kumar, who had taught the lovers to dream, was the firebrand of the youth. He had bid farewell to us, thereafter he was not seen at all. Fighting with the infinite problems in his life, he had set out to find a job with his coconut-climbing machine. He had a fall from the coconut tree one day and broke his thigh. He was bedridden with paralysis below his waist. All the wild roads were asphalted then.

Satheesh had spoken eloquently about his life for almost an hour. We could read the same agility in his eyes as it had been during the valedictory day at the college. We climbed down Muthukad hill opening a new friendship.

My confidence level was going up after I met with Satheesh. Since then I continued my physical exercise with hard work. I could walk about 159 steps without assistance. Once I fell on the courtyard and injured.

X-ray result showed that there was a fracture on the right big toe. I couldn't walk for three weeks. It was a bit disappointing, but there came the happy news that brought my vigour up. Two friends were ready to produce my gazals into an album. They were the senior batch of students at CKGM College.

Even when I was a man with progressive ideology, divine threads and talisman had to be worn due to the pressure of my friends and my mother. Today too, mother brought a hallowed talisman to be worn around one of my hands. My philosophy was getting thinner because of the increasing presence of religious rituals. From Nadapuram, known as the land of the hot-tempered, news came that people clashed among themselves, looting neighbours, burning houses, killing each other, etc.

It was a day of bandh here. Therefore, I could visit the hospital for removing plaster next day. The doctors advised me to complete rest for two more weeks. I had a fear that if exercises were discontinued it would affect my physique. I did simple physical exercises on the bed and gave more thrust to the training of my fingers. Though the letters were not so beautiful, I was able to write with a pen.

I didn't seriously notice the passage of three weeks with plaster on my feet.

During the daytime, I fell back into the life of a recluse to concentrate wholly on writing. Apart from gazals, the story 'Chambamaram' got much appreciation in social media sites. After 21 days, the plaster was removed. The wounds had completely healed. As the walking exercises had stopped completely, the feet didn't get momentum. It was with great caution that Hussain started physiotherapy this time.

It seemed that I had lost confidence in walking without assistance. Yet, without losing my mental courage, I resumed walking exercise.

After what seemed to be a hard task for three days, the legs and feet got back the previous momentum. February 14 was Saturday, on which date was the recording my gazals at a Koyilandy studio. I waited for Anash, Shaneesh, and Vinod Pandiri. We reached Koyilandy at one o'clock.

The studio was on the second floor of an old building behind Krishna Cinema. To take me up 42 stairs, they had to take much effort. I didn't notice the pain or difficulties in climbing up the stairs, out of my excitement to reach the studio. Advocate Vineesh and singer Anagha had started their mission in the morning itself. Having lunch at Koyilandy and after listening to the sound recording of 'Pathirakkattu', we returned while darkness began to spread outside the studio.

The outside scenes looking from the vehicle seemed to be more beautiful than before. My confidence level increased. I leaned back against the seat enjoying the speedy sights going behind the vehicle.

With the exercise of my legs and feet, I had started to move the fingers myself. The fingers are moving better now. Sajeesh Kayalad had asked me to prepare a page on Facebook to advertise about the album which I did soon. The letters were not so legible. 'What the flower trees of CKG have to say', 'Stepping on Podippil School again' were the two pages from which I began to send messages of my ideas. From such messages, I could bring responses in favour of me among the common people who used Facebook.

While on the one side the album work was progressing, I continued my physical exercises. Though a little more frightened, along with Hussain I stepped on to the pathway to my house. Due to the increased confidence, my legs got more agility. All the efforts of the album came to an optimistic conclusion. The premiere edition of the songs climbed down into my eardrums under the mango tree of my courtyard.

When I listened to my lines as songs, my delight had its culmination.

Again, the control of my body was undertaken by the brain. The fingers began to design and interconnect words along with the mind. The footsteps became strong with the poetic mind filled with poems, stories, etc.

The last paragraphs were written in my handwriting. During the waning breath of my life, I met a friend on the way and she penned down my words silently with delight. She was waiting for finishing the little autobiography of mine at the friendly shore of Kozhikode. I set out in the early morning, after breakfast and wearing new clothes. My friend Suneesh Kilayil was the leader.

The summer shower began to fall on the earth giving a chill to nature and my mind. Sights being moved behind, the car slowly gained momentum, emitting smoke along the Mundakkutty road, and filling my mind with ecstasy.

# 17. On the shore of my love

ONE DAY while I was immersed in my journey through beautiful imaginations, I got a surprise call on my mobile phone.

"Rasith bhai, kaisa hai?" VGP was on the phone!

"Hope you are doing fine. I read your Facebook post, listened to your album too. They are very nice and wonderful. Are you planning to publish a book?"

"Yes, sir. I have a plan."

"Okay. Do you have any idea what Guillain-Barre syndrome (GBS) is?"

"Only a little, sir."

"Then, let me explain. GBS is a rare but serious autoimmune disorder. Here the immune system attacks healthy nerve cells in your peripheral nervous system. This leads to weakness, numbness, and tingling. It can eventually cause paralysis. The cause of this particular condition is unknown, but it's typically triggered by an infectious illness, such as the stomach flu or a lung infection. I think, in your case you had a stomach upset before consulting the hospital in Mysuru."

"Exactly, sir."

He resumed the talk and I listened to him carefully.

"GBS affects only about 1 in 10,00,000 people. You cannot find an exact cure for GBS, but treatment can reduce the severity of the symptoms and shorten the duration of the illness. In GBS, your immune system attacks the peripheral nervous system that connects your brain to the rest of your body and transmits signals to your muscles. The muscles will not be able to respond to signals they receive from your brain if these nerves are damaged. The first symptom is usually a tingling sensation in your toes, feet and legs. The tingling spreads upward to your arms and fingers. The symptoms can usually progress very rapidly. In some people, the disease can become serious in just a few hours as happened in your case."

I was completely silent. And I stood as if in a reverie listening to his voice.

He explained further.

"The symptoms of GBS include difficulty moving your eyes or face, talking, chewing or swallowing, severe lower back pain, loss of bladder control, fast heart rate, difficulty in breathing and paralysis. It is difficult to diagnose it at first. It is because the symptoms are very similar to those of other neurological disorders or conditions that affect the nervous system, such as botulism, heavy metal poisoning or meningitis. That is why your doctors at Mysuru hospital were unable to tell you what it was. The symptoms can quickly get worse and can be fatal if they aren't treated. In severe cases, people with GBS can develop full-body paralysis. GBS can be life-threatening if paralysis affects the diaphragm or chest muscles, preventing proper breathing.

"In general, symptoms will get worse for two to four weeks before they stabilise. Recovery can then take anywhere from a few weeks to a few years. People with GBS usually recover in six to 12 months.

"There are some interesting developments about this disease which were revealed recently. A Michigan State University research team is the first to show how a common bacterium found in improperly cooked chicken causes GBS.

"The research published in the *Journal of Autoimmunity* demonstrates how this food-borne bacterium, known as *Campylobacter jejuni*, triggers GBS, and it also offers new information for a cure. If chicken isn't cooked to the proper minimum internal temperature, bacteria can still exist. It is seen that treatment with some antibiotics could make the disease worse. Scientists share a new concern related to an increase of the disease due to the Zika virus too. There are many other bacteria and viruses associated with GBS. In the journal, Linda Mansfield says about the causes of the disease and the possible cure too."

He disconnected the phone after the usual exchange of greetings. I was amazed to listen to his words about GBS.

The disease has given me a new life, a life away from the unpredictable dreariness, a life with more energy and vitality. I realized it has become a turning point in my life. I have sprung up with rebirth from the dilapidated hallucination of the garden city. I cannot live a life of futility. I am coming back.

Abandoning unwanted thoughts indefatigably, through the deeply intimate friendship of music, along the sublime terrain of love, I am coming back.

Thank You Guillain-Barre Syndrome!

# Rasith Asokan

Author Rasith Asokan, born April 19, 1981, is an Indian author and lyricist. He is a bestselling author of the Malayalam book *Nanni...Guillain-Barre Syndrome*. The book has been reprinted 22 times, and over 25 thousand copies have been sold and distributed. The English edition *Thank You Guillain-Barre Syndrome* is published by Winco Books India.

Mob: 9645031372. Email: rasithasok@gmail.com

**Books and Albums**

- *Nanni...Guillain-Barre Syndrome* (Life -experience, 22 editions).
- *Kalankode Colony* (Story, 6 editions).
- *Chuvarezhuthu* (Poetry, 2 editions).
- *Annu Ninakkayi* (Album, sold 12,000 copies) Sung by friends. Lyrics by Rasith Asokan.
- *Violet Flowers for You* (Album). Sung by famous playback singers P. Jayachandran and Sujatha Mohan, Sithara Krishnakumar and Nishad along with friends. Lyrics by Rasith Asokan.

**Awards**

- *Nanni...Guillain-Barre Syndrome* won the State Award of the Department of Social Welfare for the year 2015-16.
- Varam 2017 Story Award for short story *Moy Sameedas.*
- Literary Award 2019 for the story *Buljureshiyil Viriyunna Chembarathi Poovukal.*

22nd EDITION

# നന്ദി ഗില്ലൻ ബാരി സിൻഡ്രോം

രാസിത്ത് അശോകൻ

കാലങ്കോട്
കോളനി
രാസിത്ത് അശോകൻ

ചുവരെഴുത്ത്
രാസിത്ത് അശോകൻ
DCB

# Yoosaph Perambra

The translator Dr. Yoosaph A.K. aka Yoosaph Perambra, Asst. Professor and Research Guide, lectures at the Department of English and Research Centre, Govt. College, Mokeri.

Three English books are to his credit, and he has published 4 books in the Malayalam language, apart from several articles, essays, and translations in Malayalam as well as in English. Currently, he lives in Kozhikode District of Kerala State.

www.ingramcontent.com/pod-product-compliance
Ingram Content Group UK Ltd.
Pitfield, Milton Keynes, MK11 3LW, UK
UKHW042015190726
13854UKWH00005B/2299